ENGLISH G

access 5

WORKBOOK

Vokabel Trainer Cornelsen

Vokabeltrainer-App

Verfügbar für: iOS, Android und Windows Phone

scook

AUDIOS online

Deine **interaktiven Gratis-Übungen** und **Audios** findest du auf scook.de. Dort gibst du den unten stehenden Zugangscode in die Box ein.

Dein Zugangscode auf www.scook.de | mv2hd-v3pdg

Cornelsen

Australia, country and continent

Die interaktive Übung 1 findest du auf www.scook.de. Zum Einloggen auf Scook brauchst du den Code auf Seite 1.

1 Welcome to Australia! → SB (p. 10–11) • Wordbank 1

Look carefully at the two pictures of Australia. What do they tell you about the country and about the life there? Which picture do you prefer, and why? Write down your ideas.

1

2

Picture 1

2 REVISION Have you made many friends yet? (Simple past or present perfect) ➜ SB (p. 14) • GF 1.4

Put the sentences in the two dialogues in the right order. Choose the correct form of the verbs in brackets ( ).

☐ Yes, I have. It ______ (be) hard at first, but I ______ (meet) some nice kids when I ______ (join) the rugby team.

☐ Not yet, but nobody ______ (organize) any so far – it's still October, so we ______ (even not celebrate) Halloween!

☐ ______ (you make) any friends at your new school yet?

☐ ______ (already they invite) you to any Christmas parties?

☐ Oh yeah, we ______ (go) there too. I ______ (buy) a cool T-shirt at the market.

☐ ______ (you have) a good time in Sydney last week?

☐ I ______ (never be) there. When we ______ (go) to Sydney, we ______ (stay) in The Rocks.

☐ It ______ (be) amazing. We ______ (stay) in … er … Woolloomooloo. I ______ (still not learn) how to say it correctly!

3 REVISION A conversation in Sydney (Simple present and present progressive) ➜ SB (p. 14) • GF 1.4

Put the verbs in brackets ( ) into the correct form: simple present or present progressive.

Assistant: Hi. *Are you looking* (you look) for anything special?

Student: Oh, hello. I ______ (try) to find an Australian souvenir for my mum. She ______ (live) in Germany.

Assistant: Wow, you're really far from home. ______ (you learn) English here?

Student: Yes. I ______ (do) a high school programme.

Assistant: People here ______ (always not learn) German at school, so I guess your English ______ (get) better really quickly. Here we ______ (learn) Japanese and Mandarin as well as European languages.

Student: Yes, I ______ (go) to a beginners' Japanese class every afternoon after school. They ______ (give) us a lot of homework – it's quite tiring. So I ______ (really enjoy) my free day today!

Assistant: Oh, my boss ______ (call) me. I'd better go. Nice talking to you!

4 WORDS Australia puzzle ➜ SB (p. 15)

Write the words in the puzzle. What's the word in the blue boxes?

1 quiet part of the sea, with land around it

2 friend

3 connected with native Australians

4 connected with town or city

5 opposite of dry

6 difficult to reach

➜ _ _ _ _ _ _

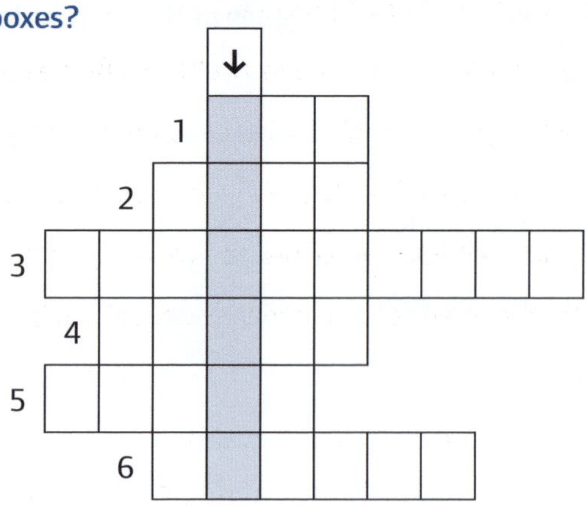

5 Australian sounds ➜ SB (p. 15) • SF 22 (p. 71)

a) ○ 02 Listen and write the sentences.

1 ______________________________

2 ______________________________

3 ______________________________

4 ______________________________

b) 03 Listen to the sentences. Are the people speaking British or Australian English? Write BE or AusE.

1	________	3	________	5	________	7	________
2	________	4	________	6	________	8	________

6 Discover Manly ➜ SB (p. 15) • SF 12–15 (pp. 69–70)

04 Listen to the guide. You go on a tour of Manly in Sydney. Your German friend wants to know what you saw and did there. Take notes below about what you saw and think about what you did there. Then write an email in German in your exercise book to your friend back home.

____

____

____

____

7 REVISION About The Rocks (Relative clauses: *who* or *which*) ➜ *SB (p. 16) • GF 7 (pp. 84–85)*

○ (Circle) the correct relative pronoun.

1 The people **which** / (**who**) lived in The Rocks first were the Gadigal Aboriginals.

2 Then convicts – people **which** / **who** had done something wrong in England – arrived.

3 The houses **which** / **who** these new Australians built were large and comfortable.

4 Not all convicts **which** / **who** wanted to marry could find a wife.

5 A guided tour is often recommended for people **which** / **who** visit The Rocks.

6 Something **which** / **who** surprises a lot of visitors is the streets: they're not straight.

7 There are a lot of lively markets and shops **which** / **who** are popular with tourists.

8 Jewellery, clothes and art are just some of the things **which** / **who** visitors can buy.

8 REVISION Fun at Manly Beach (Participle clauses instead of relative clauses) ➜ *SB (p. 16) • GF 8.2 (p. 86)*

a) ○ Use a participle clause to make one sentence out of two. Write the sentences in your exercise book.

1 Near the water there is a group of children. They are having a surfing lesson.

Near the water there is a group of children having a surfing lesson.

2 Outside the café there is a tiny dog. It is drinking from a dish of water.

3 Inside there is a teenage boy. He's buying an ice cream.

4 Look at that woman. She's running into the sea with a surfboard.

5 A girl is filming her friend. He is trying to stand up on his surfboard.

6 Behind her friend is a very good surfer. He's riding a huge wave.

7 An old man is walking past some tourists. They're taking silly photos.

b) ● Order the words to make sentences with participle clauses. Write the sentences in your exercise book.

1 a · beach · watching · man · on · there's · kitesurfers · the · the

There's a man on the beach watching the kitesurfers.

2 sitting · a · reading · tree · there's · book · a · a · under · woman

3 playing · beach · are · there · some · boys · on · football · the

4 for · the · there · café · birds · are · near · food · looking

9 REVISION Make sentences … (Participle clauses after verbs of perception) ➜ *SB (p. 16) • GF 8.3 (p. 86)*

Use the verbs to make sentences about the pictures. Use participle clauses and write in your exercise book.

1

I noticed a dog taking a child's ice cream.

2

3

4
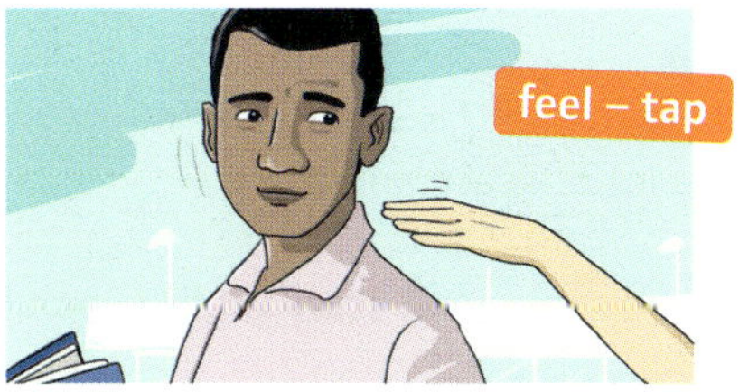

5

10 STUDY SKILLS Argumentative writing ➜ SB (p. 17) • SF 9 (p. 67)

a) ○ Underline the correct answer.

1 In an argumentative text you: present only your arguments / present only arguments that you don't agree with / present arguments for and against a topic

2 You form your opinion: before you start / after you have collected ideas and arguments / after you have written the text

3 You structure your content: before you collect ideas / before you start writing / while you are writing

4 You use special expressions to: start each paragraph / talk about your experiences / explain your opinion in every paragraph

b) Now write an argumentative text in your exercise book. Follow the five steps on page 17 of your student's book. Steps 3 and 4 give you some examples of expressions you can use. Your topic is: "Australians don't need to learn foreign languages." The ideas in the table can help you to start:

For	Against
– English is a world language; you can speak it everywhere – …	– not everyone in the world speaks English – …

11 WORDS A year in Far North Queensland ➜ SB (p. 18–19)

Complete the text about 16-year-old Katharina's experience as an exchange student in Far North Queensland.

I had heard a lot about 'FNQ', but nothing could really prepare for that moment when my **f** ____________ landed and I went outside into the warm, **h** ____________ air. Living in Cape Trib, I mainly experienced **r** ____________ – not **u** ____________ – Australia. There weren't many **t** ____________ cafés or **b** ____________ **d** ____________ with skyscrapers here – just **r** ____________ **r** ____________ with a lot of space and **s** ____________ landscapes, like coral **r** ____________. The **e** ____________ and sometimes scary wildlife soon became an everyday sight for me: **p** ____________ **s** ____________, **p** ____________ and **i** ____________ everywhere. One day I even saw a **c** ____________ while I was **s** ____________ at the beach – **l** ____________ it didn't see me! The best thing about the year was all the Aussies I met. I **b** ____________ **i** ____________ the same people all the time, because we lived in a small town. With **m** ____________ who were so **t** ____________ and **e** ____________, how could I ever be homesick?

12 After dinner … (Participle clauses) ➜ SB (p. 20) • GF 8 (pp. 85–87)

a) ○ Rewrite the sentences, using a participle clause.

1 After dinner we sat outside and listened to the insects and birds.

After dinner sat outside, ~~listened~~ listening to the insects and birds.

2 The frog stayed inside and tried to hide from the python.

Frog stayed inside, trying to hide from the Python.

3 I swam away from the crocodile and hoped it hadn't seen me.

Swam away from the crocodile, hoping it hadn't seen me.

4 A big moth flew around my bedroom and made me very nervous.

A big moth flew around my bedroom, making me very nervous

b) Match the sentence beginnings to the pictures. Then finish each sentence with a participle clause.

3

1

2

1 Mark sat on a piece of wood, chilling his life.

2 Look at the people, surfinge in the sea

3 This is us on holiday, sitting on our car.

13 While packing for our trip … (Participle clauses with *while* and *when*) ➜ SB (p. 21) • GF 8.5 (p. 87)

Use participle clauses to join each pair of sentences. Use when or while in the participle clause.

1	**a** We packed for our trip to Australia.	**b** We got more and more excited.
2	**a** We found some cool places to stay.	**b** We looked online for information.
3	**a** I fell off my board lots of times.	**b** I learned to surf.
4	**a** We visited The Rocks.	**b** We spent hours at the markets.
5	**a** I filmed the river.	**b** I provoked a 6 m-long crocodile.

1 *While packing for our trip to Australia, we got more and more excited.*

2 While looking online for information, we found some cool places to stay

3 While learning ~~sur~~ to surf, I fell off my board lots of times.

4 While they spending hours at the market, we visited the rocks

5 While filming the river, provoke a 6-m long crocodile

14 A terrible day at school ➔ SB (p. 21) • SF 3–5 (pp. 64–66)

● Write a short text (about 150 words) in your exercise book about a bad day at school, using participle clauses. These ideas can help you:

While riding my bike to school, I lost my phone …/In the art lesson I dropped paint all over my legs, destroying my jeans …/My maths teacher stood outside the classroom, looking angry …

15 EXTRA Coming from Sydney … (Using participle clauses to give reasons) ➔ SB (p. 21) • GF 8.6 (p. 87)

Rewrite the sentences, using participle clauses to explain the reasons.

1 We come from Sydney, which is why we find the weather in FNQ strange.

Coming from Sydney, we find the weather in FNQ strange.

2 I have red hair. That's why I always have to put on a lot of sunscreen.

____

3 I passed my driving test when I was 15 because I lived in the USA.

____

4 I heard a loud voice at the door, so I knew my friend was here.

____

5 I wanted to buy ice cream, which is why I stopped at the supermarket.

____

16 ACCESS TO WORDS Nature[1] in Australia ➔ SB (p. 22)

You are going to prepare words to help you talk about Australia's landscape and wildlife. Then you will give a one-minute talk about nature in Australia. Use your exercise book.

a) **Word field:** landscape and wildlife. Structure the vocabulary in the box, using a method you know (e. g. table, mind map, …). You can add more words if you like.

> ant · bay · beach · bird · bush · camel · climate · coastline · coral reef · crocodile · flying fox · flood · inland · insect · kangaroo · koala · moth · mountain · ocean · outback · palm tree · python · rain · rainforest · remote · region · river · rock · rural · snake · spider · tree frog · wave

b) **Adjectives:** Look at the words in the box. Find pairs that have opposite meanings, e. g. busy – remote. How many pairs can you find?

> boring · busy · calm · cold · coastal · dangerous · dry · exotic · flat · hot · inland · humid · lonely · marine · mild · mountainous · nearby · overcrowded · poisonous · relaxing · remote · rocky · rural · safe · scary · sandy · tiny · tropical · scenic · urban · vast · wet

c) **Verbs:** Which nouns from a) could you use with these verbs? bite · provoke · swim · bump into · flood · injure

d) ● Prepare a one-minute talk or a page with pictures and a text for your class about Australia's landscape and wildlife. Before you start, make a list of twelve words you want to use.

[1] nature ['neɪtʃə] *Natur*

17 SPEAKING COURSE Agreeing and disagreeing → SB (p. 23)

a) ○ Write three phrases you can use to give your opinion.

1 ______ 2 ______ 3 ______

b) ○ Write three expressions you can use to agree with someone.

1 ______ 2 ______ 3 ______

c) The following three expressions are used to disagree with someone, but they are very direct. Add extra phrases to make them more polite (look at Step 3 on p. 23 of your student's book).

1 That's nonsense. ______

2 I don't agree. ______

3 That's not how I see it. ______

d) Think about the following statements and tick (✓) the correct boxes.

When you disagree with someone in English you …

1 need to make your opinion clear, so you should start with a short answer like "No". ☐
2 can sometimes use expressions like "That's rubbish!" without being rude. ☐
3 should remember that some people can disagree strongly with you even when they sound polite. ☐
4 will sound more polite if you're direct. ☐
5 should explain your opinion after you have given it. ☐
6 shouldn't show any understanding for the other person's opinion, because then your argument isn't clear. ☐

e) ● Write three sentences agreeing and three sentences disagreeing with each statement. Give reasons. Look at expressions on p. 23 of your student's book. Use your sentences in class when discussing the statements.

1 "Towns would be much nicer if cars weren't allowed."
2 "Birds make better pets than cats or dogs."
3 "Money can't buy happiness."

______
______
______
______
______
______
______
______
______

18 EXTRA BACKGROUND FILE The Aboriginal people ... ➔ SB (pp. 24–25)

Read the text about Australia's Aboriginal people on pp. 24–25 of your student's book again.

a) ○ Underline the correct answer.

1 Australia's Aboriginal people: have lived in Australia for over 50,000 years / originally came from Asia / are the world's oldest civilisation.

2 Aboriginal people were: farmers / hunters and gatherers / spiritual leaders / ready to learn about European cultures.

3 Aboriginal people taught their children about their traditions: by teaching them all the different languages / through paintings / through songs and chants.

4 Songlines: were invented so that people could trade / show how important the landscape was for Aboriginal people / didn't work in every language.

b) ● Write down the answers.

1 Explain how a songline helps people to travel without maps. ______________________

____

2 Why did the Aboriginal population fall between 1788 and 1900? Give two reasons. ______________________

____

3 Who are the "Stolen Generations"? ______________________

____

4 Name two things that show that people in Australia are sorry about what happened to the Stolen Generations.

____

____

c) ● Describe how life in Australia was for Aboriginal people in 1900, and how it is different now. Write about 150 words in your exercise book.

In 1900 Aboriginal people didn't have ...

19 WORDS Leon's email ➔ SB (p. 25)

Complete Leon's email about his trip to Far North Queensland.

Hi Steve! I'm in FNQ with Brian, Elvira and Nick, and you were **t** __________ right – it's an awesome **r** __________ ! **L** __________ , it's the dry season, so there are no **f** __________ . We've seen some **c** __________ – **m** __________ in the river. I'm **d** __________ see a **p** __________ , but Brian doesn't want to **b** __________ any snakes at our campsite – he'd **p** __________ to go to the zoo, so that's what we're going to do. The campsite is OK. It has great **f** __________ , but it's **o** __________ at the moment because it's the holidays. We're **s** __________ a bathroom with about 100 other people! Anyway, I have to go – we're planning a **s** __________ trip to a coral **r** __________ .

See you soon, **m** __________ ! Leon

20 The Australian of the Year awards ➜ *SB (p. 28) • SF 12–15 (pp. 69–70)*

● 05 You listen to a German podcast about the "Australian of the Year" competition. You need the information for a one-minute talk in English.

a) Write notes in your exercise book.

Explain:
- what the Australian of the Year Awards are.
- when the winners receive their awards.
- why the awards are important for Australia.
- what kind of people win (giving an example of what someone did).
- what makes the awards unusual.

b) Practise giving a one-minute talk about the Australian of the Year competition.

21 Life in Kintore (Past participle clauses) ➜ *SB (p. 28) • GF 8.7 (p. 87)*

Rewrite the sentences with past participle clauses. Write in your exercise book.

1 Kintore is a community that was founded in 1981, when many Pintupi people moved there from Papunya.
Kintore is a community founded in 1981, when many Pintupi people moved there from Papunya.

2 In 2011, when they were asked for a government study what group they belonged to, 91 per cent said they were Aboriginal.

3 Pintupi is the name of the group and of the language that is spoken in Kintore.

4 There is a group of artists from Kintore who are known for their special style of painting.

5 In the past, the paintings that were made by the group always sold for a lot of money.

6 Bush turkeys are just one kind of animals which are hunted when the Pintupi people go out bush.

7 "The Honey Ant dreaming" is a story that is told to kids around the fire.

8 The band Midnight Oil sang about Kintore in "Beds are Burning", a famous song which was described as the third-best Australian song of all time.

22 An Australian rock band (Present and past participle clauses) ➜ *SB (p. 28) • GF 8 (pp. 85–87)*

Choose the correct participle: present or past.

1 Midnight Oil were an Australian rock band also ____________ (know) as "The Oils".

2 The band was founded in 1972, originally ____________ (perform) under the name "Farm".

3 When ____________ (study) in Canberra, the singer, Peter Garret, answered an ad to Join Farm – and the rest is history.

4 To choose their new name, the band wrote ideas on pieces of paper and put them in a hat, ____________ (pull) out "Midnight Oil" by chance.

5 "Beds are Burning" (1987) is a song still ____________ (play) by radio stations all around the world today.

6 When ____________ (ask) to play at the 2000 Sydney Olympics, the band agreed – and decided to use their performance to raise awareness[1] of the suffering of the Aboriginal people.

[1] awareness [ə'weənəs] *Bewusstsein*

1 WORDS Australia and the UK

Complete the sentences with words from this unit in the correct form.

The UK and Australia have many things in common, even ______________ they are very different countries – one ______________ and ______________, and one tiny and, some might say, ______________. The two countries ______________ some of their history and culture because parts of Australia were ______________ by British colonists, including ______________. ______________, the colonists killed many ______________ people, but since the 1990s, citizens' movements have worked hard to recognise the native people's suffering. Today there are many ______________ between the UK and Australia. Young Brits or ______________ who want to try living ______________ can work in each other's country for a year or two. It's a very long ______________, but when they get there young British people like the ______________ lifestyle, ______________ landscape and ______________ wildlife of Australia. Many young Australians are interested in exploring the UK, with its ______________ towns, ______________ climate and famous ______________.

2 AusE pronunciation

06 **Listen and write the sentences.**

1 ______________________________

2 ______________________________

3 ______________________________

4 ______________________________

3 An Aussie in London (Participle clauses)

Complete the text with the correct present and past participles. Use the verbs from the box.

ask · be · believe · cheer · clap · come · film · forget · help · pull · take · turn · walk · work · visit

Mark left Sydney to spend time in London *working* in a café. ~~Lost~~ Asking ______________ Australian, he is allowed to work in the UK for two years. It's a café often visiting ______________ by tourists, so there are usually young people from all over the world taking ______________ selfies in the street outside. Many of them stand in the road, forgetting ______________ that cars in the UK drive on the left. Once, while walking ______________ to work, Mark noticed two Spanish girls filming ______________ each other in the road. Suddenly, he heard a car coming ______________. The girls didn't look at it, hoping ______________ that they weren't in danger. Mark acted quickly, pulling ______________ them away from the road. People saw him helping ______________ the girls. Soon, there was a crowd of people cheering ______________ and claping ______________. Mark didn't like that. The girls' video shows his face turning ______________ red! But when ______________ about it later by his boss, Mark felt quite proud.

4 What are they doing? (Listening for gist)

07 Listen to Olivia and her English friend Harry. What are they doing? Tick (✓) a box.

1 A ◯ Walking through flood water B ◯ Learning to surf C ◯ Taking a ferry to Manly

2 A ◯ Shopping in The Rocks B ◯ Watching an Australian Rules Football match C ◯ Going on a tour of Sydney CBD

5 A conversation at the beach (Listening for gist and detail)

a) 08 Listen to Megan, Finn and Zoe. What are they talking about? Circle A, B or C.

A A trip to England **B** Plans for an exchange year **C** Differences between Australia and the UK

b) 08 Read the questions. Then listen again and write short answers (1–6 words).

1 Which other cities will Finn travel through on his trip from Sydney to Glasgow? ______

2 How long will Finn's trip take? ______

3 Why does Megan think Finn will get a shock? ______

4 Why won't Finn miss his family? Give two reasons. ______

5 What will Finn miss most of all? ______

6 When was the host family's house built? ______

7 Why is Finn not sure that he has the right information about the family? ______

8 Why does Zoe think Finn's host parents might be strict? ______

9 What must Finn do in Glasgow? Name three things. ______

10 How many kilometres is Glasgow from Sydney? ______

Check: Listening

a) Vergleiche deine Antworten mit den Lösungen auf Seite 88 im Workbook.
b) Schätze deine Antworten mit einem grünen oder roten Gesicht ein.

	☺	☹	
1 Hast du in Aufgabe 2 die Sätze ohne Probleme verstehen und aufschreiben können?	◯	◯	➔ 1
2 Hast du in den Aufgaben 4/1 und 4/2 verstanden, was die Sprecher machen?	◯	◯	➔ 3, 4a, 5a
3 Hast du in 5a) problemlos verstanden, worüber die Freunde sich unterhalten?	◯	◯	➔ 3, 4a, 5a
4 Hast du in 5b) die Detailfragen ohne Probleme richtig beantworten können?	◯	◯	➔ 4b, 5b
5 Hast du in 5b) die Zahlen und Daten problemlos verstanden?	◯	◯	➔ 2

c) Wenn du dich rot eingeschätzt hast, schau dir die rechte Spalte an.
Die Nummern führen dich zu den passenden Übungen im Skills Training (S. 14–15).
Dort kannst du gezielt Listening trainieren.

1 WORDS Understanding AusE ➜ SF 22 (p. 71)

09 Listen and repeat the words and phrases you hear. Then write them down.

1 ______ 6 ______
2 ______ 7 ______
3 ______ 8 ______
4 ______ 9 ______
5 ______ 10 ______

TIP: Some words sound different in BE and AusE. Expect to hear differences in words like:
- light, look, leave
- letter, butter
- price, why, night
- stairs, care, where
- village, women
- next, pet, send
- cart, star, afternoon
- tea, seat

2 Numbers ➜ SF 22 (p. 71)

10 Listen and write what you hear as a number.

1 ______ 4 ______ 7 ______
2 ______ 5 ______ 8 ______
3 ______ 6 ______ 9 ______

TIP: Remember these examples:
- 86 = **eighty**-six
- thirt**een** (13), thirt**y** (30)
- 2001: two thousand and one.

3 Radio programmes (Listening for gist) ➜ SF 22 (p. 71)

11 Noah is deciding which radio programmes to listen to. What are they about? Read the topics. Then listen once. Write the number of the programme (1–4) in the correct box.

☐ Young people who are leaving school
☐ "Australian of the Year" winners
☐ Animals from around the world
☐ Job advice for teenagers
☐ Life without the Internet
☐ People who've done something great
☐ Helping Australian wildlife
☐ Teenagers who don't use technology

TIP: Listen only once for **gist** (the **general meaning**), not for details. Ask yourself **what it is about**. Look at the topics. Which words would you expect to hear? Listen for those **key words**.

For example:
Animals from around the world → countries, live, feed.

4 An Australian animal (Listening for gist and detail) ➜ SF 22 (p. 71)

a) 12 Which animal are they talking about? Listen once. Then circle A, B, C or D.

A crocodile

B cassowary

C bush turkey

D camel

b) 12 Read the questions. Then listen again. Are the statements true or false? Tick (✓) T or F after each statement.

	T	F
1 Adult animals of this kind can be more than 2 metres tall.	◯	◯
2 If it was provoked, the baby animal would attack.	◯	◯
3 These animals use their toes to defend themselves.	◯	◯
4 These animals can run at 50 km/hour, but they can't swim.	◯	◯
5 These animals are nervous around humans.	◯	◯
6 These animals are vegetarian.	◯	◯
7 At the zoo they are fed fruit.	◯	◯
8 The modern world can be dangerous for these animals.	◯	◯
9 Dogs sometimes attack them.	◯	◯
10 In Queensland people are working to help these animals.	◯	◯

TIP: Find and mark **key words** and **key phrases** in the statements. Then listen for them or for similar expressions when you listen a second time. Check numbers and dates carefully.

5 Tourist tips (Listening for gist and detail) ➜ SF 22 (p. 71)

a) 13 What is the conversation about? Listen once. Then circle A, B or C.

TIP: Before you listen, look at the **pictures**. They can make understanding the situation quicker and easier.

A Tours of The Rocks

B Tours of Sydney

C Photography tours

b) 13 Read the questions. Then listen again and write short answers (1–6 words).

1 Who does Tim know from Perth? __________

2 How many hours does it take to drive from Perth to Sydney? __________

3 How many countries in the world are larger than Australia? __________

4 Why isn't Tim staying in Woolloomooloo? __________

5 What kind of areas does Tim like to visit when he is travelling? __________

6 How did he learn to use his camera? __________

7 What is special about the architect tours? __________

8 What does the building at 1 Bligh Street do with its used water? __________

9 Why does Tim think the price of the Manly bike tour is good? __________

10 Why would Aiden prefer the architect tour? __________

TIP:
1 Before you listen a second time, mark **key words** in the questions. Then listen for those words or words that mean something similar.
2 Write your answers as notes, not full sentences.

Relationships

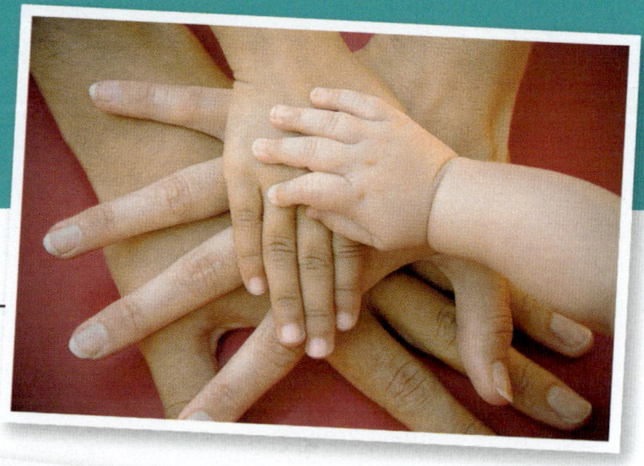

1 Relationships in pictures ➜ SB (pp. 34–35) • SF25 (pp. 72–73)

a) ○ Choose a photo and describe it in your exercise book.
Write four or more sentences.

This photo shows … On the left/In the centre you can see …

b) ● What kind of relationship is shown in the photo? Write four or more sentences in your exercise book.

The photo shows a relationship between …

c) ● If the photo was used in an advert, what kind of product or company do you think it might promote? Give reasons. Then prepare a one-minute talk about the photo for your class.

I think this photo could be used to promote …

2 WORDS A puzzle ➜ SB (p. 40)

○ Complete the puzzle with words from pp. 36–39 of your student's book.
Find the word in the blue boxes.

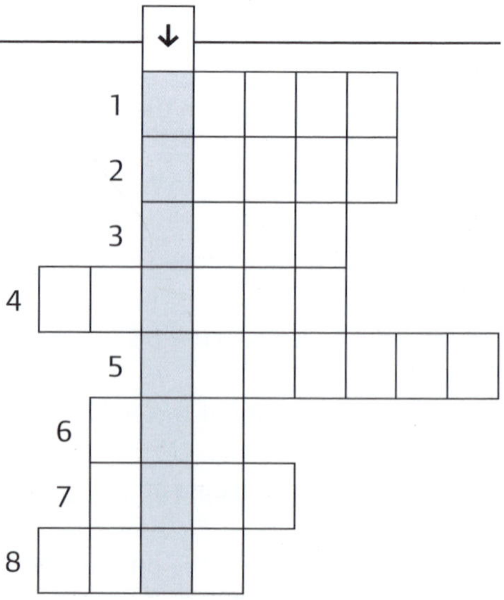

1 a topic or problem
2 a book that tells a story
3 the part of the face that's below the mouth
4 the place in the kitchen where milk and cheese are kept
5 far away
6 a part of a piano that you press to play
7 one time
something that under-18s are not usually allowed to do

… the blue boxes describes a thing that happens: _ _ _ _ _ _ _ _ _ _ .

3 He must be lonely (*must be/can't be*) ➜ SB (p. 40) • GF 4 (pp. 80–82)

Write what you would say to a friend in the following situations. Use *must be* or *can't be* with a word from the box.

awkward · easy · lonely · lucky · right · serious

Your friend…

1 says her dog barks all day when he's home alone. – **You:** He must be lonely.

2 thinks she can pass her driving test without having any lessons. You don't agree. – **You:** That ______

3 says she always wins when she plays cards with her dad. – **You:** You ______

4 won a holiday to the USA but doesn't want to go. You are surprised. – **You:** You ______

5 has to do a school project with a girl she doesn't like. – **You:** That ______

6 is learning Japanese at evening school. You think it sounds hard. – **You:** That ______

4 You can't have eaten it already! (*must have been/can't have been*) ➜ SB (p. 40) • GF 4 (pp. 80–82)

Complete B's answers. Use *must have* or *can't have* with the correct form of the verb in brackets ( ).

1 **A:** Is there any more cake left? – **B:** What? You can't have eaten (eat) that big piece already!

2 **A:** Those football fans look really happy. – **B:** But their team ______ (win). They're terrible!

3 **A:** Look at Jo on that horse – she makes it look so easy! – **B:** Yes. She ______ (ride) before.

4 **A:** Dad's car's not outside. – **B:** He ______ (drive) to the supermarket.

5 **A:** Oh no! The dog has escaped from the garden! – **B:** Don't worry. He ______ (go) far.

5 They "mustabin" ill (Compression: *must be/can't be; must have been/can't have been*) ➜ SB (p. 40) • GF 4

a) ○ 14 **Complete the sentences below. Then listen and check.**

1 They didn't come to school yesterday. They ______ ill.

2 Your mum lets you do anything! She ______ so easy-going.

3 Ed wasn't at the match yesterday. So it ______ him you saw.

4 What an amazing picture! It ______ so long to paint.

5 Lily's always talking about herself. So she ______ as shy as you think.

6 She said she didn't love him anymore. He ______ so upset.

7 Sorry I didn't phone you. I ______ the wrong number.

8 There must be some pizza left. Ben ______ it all!

b) 14 **Practise reading the sentences from a). Try to join the words in the same way. Listen and check.**

c) **Write four short statements and sentences like the ones in a). Use *must be/can't be* and *must have been/can't have been*. Then act out your sentences with a partner. Remember to join the words.**

6 REVISION Would you be able to… ? (Asking people to do things: *can, could, would*) ➜ *SB (p. 41) • GF 4*

a) ○ Match the situations to the requests.

1
You enter a café and you can't get to the only free table because a woman has put a huge shopping bag on the floor.

2
You get on the bus. You want to sit down but your friend has put his bag on the empty seat.

3
You're in a shop. You have paid but you can't pack your bag, because the man in front of you hasn't taken his bag from the packing area yet.

4
Your sister has left a bag with her dirty trainers and PE kit on your bed … again!

A
Hey, can you move your bag, please?

B
Can you move your bag?!

C
Sorry, but do you think you could take your bag, please?

D
Excuse me, could I ask you to move your bag, please?

b) Read the Access to cultures box in your student's book on p. 41 again.
Make short dialogues for the situations below. Write in your exercise book.

1 You are on the train with your friends. A man takes the seat next to you and sits on your coat.

2 You don't want to get the bus to swimming practice. You'd prefer it if your dad takes you in the car.

3 You are at the cinema and the film is about to start. You want your friend to get the seats while you get the drinks.

4 You're in your friend's garden and you kick a ball into a neighbour's garden. You knock on the neighbour's door to get the ball back.

c) Practise your dialogues with a partner.

7 REVISION Do you think we can …? (Talking about permission: *can* and *be allowed to*) ➜ *SB (p. 41) • GF 4*

a) Look at the dialogues in 4 a) on p. 41 of your student's book.
Write similar dialogues for these questions (two formal and two informal).
Write in your exercise book.

Can you …
- bring your own food into the cinema?
- get out of the car to take photos at the safari park?
- leave the exam room to have a drink or use the toilet?
- use these tickets on the tram and the bus?

b) Read the text message. Then write text messages for two of the situations from a).
Use a form of **be allowed to** in each message.

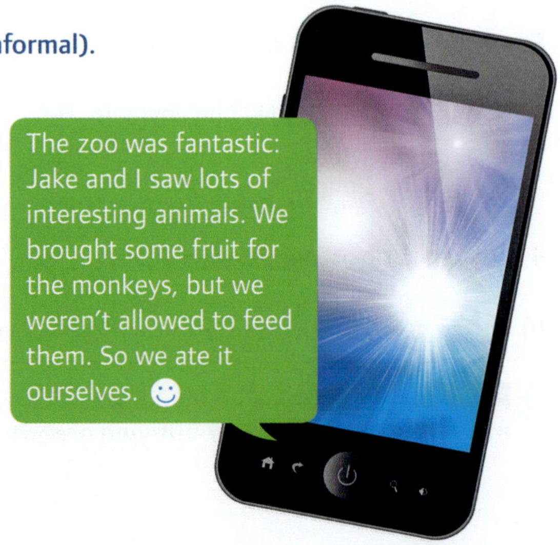

8 ACCESS TO WORDS Relationships ➜ *SB (p. 42)*

You are going to revise words to help you talk about relationships and feelings.
Then you will prepare a one-minute talk for your class about somebody you know (or a character from a film or book) who has or has had a relationship with somebody.

a) **Word field:** relationships. Choose five phrases from the box and write sentences that explain what they mean.

> break up (with sb.) · go out with sb. · be attracted to sb. · fall in love · make friends · give sb. a second chance · get to know sb. · be seeing sb. · get married · get back together · be friendly with sb. · date sb. · be furious with/at sb.

When you break up with somebody, you finish the relationship with them.

When you go out with Sb. your are dating them.
When you get back together you try a second relationship with Sb.
When you be friendly with Sb. you are kind.
When you make friends you know more people.

b) **Adjectives:** feelings. Make as many pairs of opposites as you can with words from the box.
Sometimes you can link a word with two others. Sometimes it will not be possible to find pairs.

> afraid · angry · annoyed · bored · calm · confident · confused · cross · disappointed · excited · frightened · furious · glad · glum · happy · heartbroken · hopeful · nervous · optimistic · pessimistic · pleased · relaxed · sad · scared · shocked · shy · terrified · thrilled · unhappy · upset · worried

angry =   happy = unhappy   optimistic = pessimistic
excited = calm   relaxed = worried   nervous = confident

c) **Collocations:** relationships. Write sentences in your exercise book that explain what the collocations mean.

1 Sandra is Steve's **ex-wife**.
Sandra and Steve aren't married anymore.
2 Marcus is a **family friend** of ours.
3 Joe and Julie are **old friends**.
4 Olivia has a lot of **good friends**.
5 James is my **best mate**.
6 Tom is Ella's **ex-boyfriend**.

d) ● Prepare a one-minute talk for your class about somebody you know (or a character from a film or book), who has or has had a relationship with somebody. You can also take one of the photos from this exercise and describe the relationship between the people shown.
Before you start, make a list of 8–10 words from a), b) and c) that you want to use.

9 What should they do? (German *sollen*: *should, ought to, had better*) ➔ *SB (p. 45)* • *GF 4 (pp. 80–82)*

Write what the people should and shouldn't do in the situations below. Use the phrases in the box. Write in your exercise book.

He/She should(n't) · He/She ought to … · He/She had better (not) …

1 Tim has arrived in New Zealand for his exchange year. His host family wanted to meet him at the airport, but he can't find them and his German mobile doesn't work … *Tim ought to … He shouldn't …*

2 Lukas is travelling around New Zealand, working on farms. He feels really lonely and is thinking about going home early …

3 Leah has won a trip to see her favourite band in London but if she goes, she'll miss her sister's wedding. The dates of the trip can't be changed …

4 A dog has followed Chloe home. It looks cold and hungry. She would love to bring it into the house, but her mum is allergic to dogs …

5 When Josh gets on the plane to Auckland, he realises he's forgotten to order a vegetarian meal. It's a 14-hour flight, so he will need to eat something …

6 Emily wants to leave the school basketball team because she doesn't have much free time any more, but she's the best player. If she leaves, they might stop winning matches …

10 Advice for a trip to New Zealand (German *sollen*: *be supposed to* 1) ➔ *SB (p. 45)* • *GF 4 (pp. 80–82)*

○ Use the correct form of *be supposed to* + *be* to complete these sentences.

1 You should book your flights soon. They *'re supposed to be* cheaper if you do it early.

2 You ought to change your money at the bank. It ______________ less expensive than at the airport.

3 You should visit Thames. The goldmine museum there ______________ really good.

4 You shouldn't miss Christchurch. It ______________ a really lively city.

5 You'd better not miss Kaikoura. It ______________ a fantastic place to see marine wildlife.

6 You should go to a New Zealand rugby match. They ______________ really good fun.

11 Tips for a New Zealand exchange student (Giving advice) ➔ *SB (p. 46)* • *GF 4 (pp. 80–82)*

Your friend from New Zealand is coming to your school as an exchange student. You want to give this friend some advice on how to make the most of his/her time in Germany. Write a list of eight tips in your exercise book. Use the phrases in the box and think of your own too.

- photos → hometown
- sports team → join
- practise German → me, online
- …

I think you ought to/should …
I don't think you ought to/should …

12 Advice for an exchange student in Germany (German *sollen*: *be supposed to* 2) ➜ *SB (p. 46)*

Read each pair of sentences. Then complete them using a form of **be supposed to** and **had better**.

TIP: Use **be supposed** to when talking about general rules.
Use **had better** for specific situations.

1 You *aren't supposed to be* (not be) on the train without a ticket.
You *'d better get* (get) off and buy one.

2 You ______________ (not mix) your rubbish.
You ______________ (put) the plastic in that other bin.

3 You ______________ (stop playing) that guitar.
We ______________ (not play) musical instruments here after 10 pm.

4 You ______________ (not be) late when someone invites you to their home for dinner.
We ______________ (hurry).

5 You ______________ (turn) off your mobile. We ______________ (not use) them in the cinema.

6 You ______________ (say) "Sie" to adults you don't know. I ______________ (help) you practise!

7 You ______________ (wait). We ______________ (not cross) the road when the pedestrian light is red.

13 Joining a gym (Cultural differences) ➜ *SB (p. 46)* • *SF 12–15 (pp. 69–70)*

a) Paul, an exchange student from New Zealand, wants you to help him join a gym.
Read the dialogue and make notes about what you want to say. Write in your exercise book.

Paul: I'd like to join the gym round the corner. Could you call them for me and get some information?
You: *Yes, I can call them.*
Paul: Great, thanks. Here's the phone number.
Studio: A-1 Fitness. Guten Tag. Was kann ich für Sie tun?
You: …
Studio: Wie lange hat er noch vor, in Deutschland zu bleiben?
You: …
Paul: Er … six months.
You: …
Studio: Verstehe … und wann genau möchte er trainieren?
You: …
Paul: After school and at weekends, I guess.
You: …
Studio: Gut. Ich kann ihm morgen um 17 Uhr einen Termin anbieten. Er darf für sechs Monate Mitglied werden und nachmittags ab 16 Uhr und am Wochenende trainieren. Er muss nur den Personalausweis mitbringen. Passt das?
You: …
Paul: But we don't have ID cards in New Zealand! Can I use my passport instead?
You: …
Studio: Ja, kein Problem … Für Schüler kostet die Mitgliedschaft übrigens 20 Euro pro Monat. Kann er schon morgen den ersten Monat zahlen?
You: …
Paul: Yes, that sounds great. Thanks.
You: …
Studio: Bis morgen!

b) ● 15 Listen and say your parts of the dialogue. Try not to sound too direct or unfriendly when speaking English.

c) 16 Listen and check. Were your answers similar?

14 STUDY SKILLS Statistics about internet use ➜ SB (p. 47) • SF 26 (p. 73)

a) Look at the chart below. What kind of chart is it?

It's a pie chart.

b) Complete the phrases below about the information the chart gives.
Write in your exercise book.

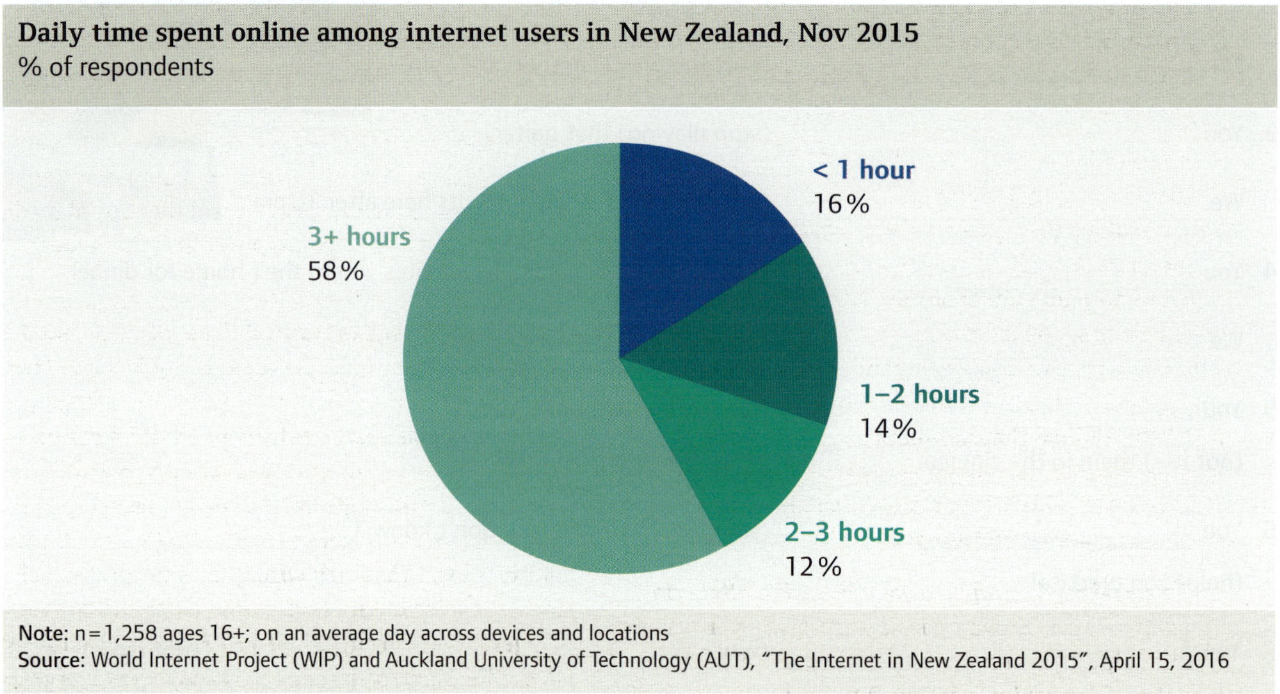

The chart is about … / It gives us information about … / The chart shows that … / If you … you can see … / My main conclusion is that …

c) ● Look at the table below. What information does it give?
Compare the five countries with each other.
Then choose four interesting facts and prepare a short talk for your class.
Make notes in your exercise book.

The table gives us information about the percentage of …

Internet users in the European Union – 2015

	Population (2015 estimate)	Number of internet users (30.11.2015)	Percentage of the country's population that uses the internet	Percentage of the EU's internet users from this country
Austria	8,584,926	7,135,168	83.1 %	1.8 %
Estonia	1,313,271	1,106,299	84.2 %	0.3 %
France	66,132,169	55,429,382	83.8 %	13.8 %
Germany	81,174,000	71,727,551	88.4 %	17.8 %
UK	64,767,115	59,333,154	91.6 %	14.7 %

Published with permission from *www.internetworldstats.com*, accessed on May 7, 2017

15 How social is social media? ➜ SB (p. 48) • SF 1–2 (p. 64)

a) Skim the text. What is it about? Write in your exercise book.

b) Read the text.

Online communication: a blessing or a curse for relationships?

The growth of the internet and social media has prompted some researchers to consider whether these communication tools make it difficult for people to form strong relationships.

A friend of mine who is a university lecturer is always complaining that young people today have worse social skills than when he was young. He says they prefer to deal with problems in writing and often avoid difficult conversations, and he believes the reason is social media: modern students just aren't used to face-to-face interaction, and this can affect their personal and professional relationships. Another friend told me that her teenage girls are constantly glued to their mobile phones, even during mealtimes, and she and her husband feel that their relationship with the girls is suffering.

Do social media really have a negative effect on relationships? Some experts warn that over-reliance on online communication is a recipe for disaster: online friendships can never be as deep as real-life ones. Plus, research shows that online relationships don't protect us as well as real-life ones do: in the past people often had one main group of friends, but now – due to social media – they usually have lots of different friends who don't know each other. This means that if you're having a difficult time and need help, your friends are less likely to notice, as they don't talk to each other.

Of course, there's no denying that online communication has its good points. In an increasingly globalised world, the internet allows us to stay connected with loved ones, no matter where they are. And whether you're a sci-fi geek or a fan of a certain band, it's never been easier to find like-minded friends. In fact, some research suggests that the internet is not destroying our relationships at all, but enriching them. If we look at teenagers, it is clear that they still value in-person contact, and the people they communicate with on social media are often people they already know and see in real life. Social media just helps them to become closer and share more experiences.

Have young people's social skills really worsened over the last couple of decades, as my lecturer friend claims? I doubt it. Society is constantly changing – and so is people's social behaviour – but I don't believe young people are more unsocial than the older generations. Older people have always complained about the younger generations – that's almost a fact of life. Plus, I think it's wrong to claim that social media use is ruining family life, as my other friend suggests. Growing up in the 1990s, I was often glued to the TV. Time spent online nowadays simply replaces time in front of the television, which is also quite an unsociable activity. Perhaps it's up to parents to set clearer rules instead of blaming social media for their problems.

I personally believe it is wrong to suggest that the internet is having a bad effect on relationships. Although there are some risks, most people manage their social interactions without any major problems. Our world is always in flux, and technologies come and go, but humans will always be social animals. It's up to us to make the best of what we have and use new tools wisely.

c) ● What are the author's opinions about …

1 whether today's young people have worse social skills than older generations?
2 whether social media is destroying family life?

Write in your exercise book.

d) Do you agree with him/her? Why (not)? Write a paragraph in your exercise book.

e) ● Summarize the article in note form and also write your opinion about the text. Then use your notes to prepare a short presentation of the text for your class. Use your exercise book.

The article is about … The author asks whether …

TIP: Try to guess the meaning of new words on your own before you look them up in a dictionary.

16 SPEAKING COURSE Having a discussion ➜ SB (p. 49)

a) How do you start, continue and end a discussion? In your exercise book, write phrases you know for:

STEP 1 (starting)
– Beginning a discussion

STEP 2 (continuing)
– giving reasons for your opinion
– supporting your argument with examples
– stressing that your arguments are strong
– interrupting another speaker
– answering when somebody interrupts you

STEP 3 (ending)
– pointing out what views you have in common
– concentrating on areas where you still don't agree
– stating your conclusions
– accepting that you aren't able to agree

– *Personally, I think ...*

b) ● You are going to prepare for a discussion in class. The topic is: "The internet solves more problems than it causes". Make a list of arguments for and against this point of view, then make notes so that you can take part in a class discussion. Remember to use the phrases you wrote for part a). Write in your exercise book.

Some points you could use are:
cyberbullying ·
practising languages ·
finding information ·
keeping in touch with friends and family

17 REVISION I would have done something else … (*would have*-form) ➜ SB (p. 52) • GF6 (p. 84)

○ Use the *would have*-form to complete the dialogues.

1 **A:** I found £100 in the street, so I bought some trainers.
B: Really? I *would have taken* (take) it to the police station.

2 **A:** The neighbours said my dog barked for hours yesterday.
B: He was probably lonely. I ____________________ (not leave) him alone all day.

3 **A:** My throat's still hurting. I can't wait to go home.
B: You poor thing. I ____________________ (not come) to school today.

4 **A:** Here, I saved a piece of birthday cake for you.
B: That's very kind of you. I ____________________ (eat) it all.

5 **A:** Ethan just texted me: he lost his passport at the beach today.
B: It's his own fault. I ____________________ (leave) it at the hostel.

6 **A:** We queued for almost three hours to get the concert tickets.
B: Wow! I ____________________ (never be) patient enough to do that.

18 If I'd spotted a celebrity (Conditional 3) ➜ SB (p. 52) • GF 6 (p. 84)

Write sentences about what you would have done if these things had happened last weekend.

1 (spot) celebrity out shopping – (take) a photo with them

If I'd spotted a celebrity out shopping, I would have taken a photo with them.

2 my parents (win) a million euros – (ask) them for a pony

3 (spend) all my money – (go) to the festival

4 (hear about) a TV programme being filmed in my street – (go) outside to watch

5 (be) offered an ice cream – (choose) strawberry flavour[1]

6 (get to know) someone interesting – (give) them my phone number

7 (meet) Alice for a coffee – (be) the first to hear her amazing news

8 (end up) doing nothing – (wait for) my friends to make plans

19 If I'd been in Ryan's situation, … (Conditional 3) ➜ SB (p. 52) • GF 6 (p. 84)

a) Ryan from England spent a month travelling in New Zealand, but his trip didn't go well. Read the text. Then write as many sentences as you can in your exercise book about what you would have done differently.

As soon as I arrived, I realised how stupid I'd been: I didn't have any New Zealand dollars, and the banks were closed on Sundays! A kind woman gave me money for the bus, so I headed for the hostel, but I couldn't remember the exact address and it took three hours to find it! On the first night I realised why it was a bad idea to share a room with nine other people – it was so noisy that I hardly slept. After four nights in this awful room I felt like I was going crazy!

I was really looking forward to my trip to Kaikoura but I got lost on the way to the bus station and missed the bus. I was so disappointed. But then two girls invited me to go to a café for lunch. Great! I left my bag on the table while I ordered my food at the counter. When I got back to the table, my laptop and camera were gone – and so were the girls! I didn't know what to do …

If I'd been in Ryan's situation, I would have changed my money.

b) Read your partner's answers and correct them if necessary.

[1] flavour ['fleɪvə] *Geschmack*

1 WORDS Refugee Action NZ

Complete the sentences with words from this unit in the correct form. Use your exercise book.

Refugee Action NZ is an (1) that supports refugees, helping them to (2) life in our country. Refugees often feel (3) and (4) when they arrive in a new place where they don't know anybody and nothing feels (5). They often have (6) problems because they don't speak English, and they may also (7) difficulties (8) the many (9) differences between their country and ours. Our (10) work with refugees to help them (11) the way things work here. The refugees we have helped have found the service (12) and say it has made them feel more (13) about building a new life here.

2 Auckland is supposed to be worth a visit (German *sollen*)

Complete the sentences with the correct English expression that means the same as German sollen. Use your exercise book.

This is what tourists in Auckland recently said:

1 You (1) stay in a hostel when you go to Auckland. They (2) be very good value.

2 **A:** Should we book a table in the Sky Tower restaurant when we arrive in Auckland?
B: No, you (3) book it before you fly – it's very popular.

3 We (4) camp here. We (5) move the tent immediately!

4 Fiordland National Park is quite far from Auckland, so they (6) keep a day free for travelling there.

5 We (7) bring jackets, because it (8) be quite cool in the winter.

6 **A:** Do you think I (9) try some adventure sports in Auckland? – **B:** No, I don't think you (10) do anything dangerous.

3 NZ tourist places

a) You are looking for information about places where you can spot marine wildlife in New Zealand. Skim the three texts. Mark the text in which you might find the answer.

b) Scan the texts to find the answers to these two questions (mark the parts):

1 What brought Europeans to Otago in the 1860s? ______________________

2 Where can you find Kauri trees? ______________________

Fiordland National Park has some of New Zealand's most amazing scenery. There is water everywhere, from the famous coastal fjords to remote waterfalls, vast lakes and rocky coastline. A popular way to explore the fjords is by sea kayak, and visitors can also enjoy a scenic flight over the park. This area is a haven for birds, with several protected species. Don't miss the Te Anau Wildlife Centre, where you can see the Takahe bird. People thought that this bird had died out, until it was rediscovered in 1948.

Queenstown is one of the country's top tourist destinations. Lake Wakatipu and the nearby snowy mountain peaks provide a stunning setting for almost every adventure sport you could imagine: why not go wild and try white-water rafting, rock climbing, mountain biking, bungee jumping or downhill skiing? It's also a great base for exploring the nearby gold-mining towns. Europeans first came here in 1853, and more arrived during the Otago gold rush of the 1860s. Today, an old 1912 riverboat is still used on the lake.

The beautiful Bay of Islands is three hours by car from Auckland and one of the country's most popular holiday destinations. You'll find the perfect activity here: from sea kayaking along the coast, to hiking the island trails, visiting the famous rock formation "Hole in the Rock" and exploring sub-tropical forests of Kauri trees. With over 144 islands, it's the perfect area for water sports and is a popular fishing spot. As well as extreme-sports fans, you might spot penguins, dolphins and whales in their natural habitat.

4 A New Zealand tradition that's all about feelings

a) Scan the text and answer questions 1–6 in your own words. Use your exercise book. First mark keywords.

1 What is a haka? Why were the first haka performed?
2 How have rugby players made haka better known?
3 How do people feel when they see a haka by the All Blacks?
4 How many views got the most popular haka?
5 Name three sad events for which haka were performed in recent years.
6 In which US sport are teams now performing haka?

What is haka?

The haka is a dance invented by the Maori people of New Zealand. It is performed by a group, with lots of quick movements and shouting. A haka dancer also makes frightening faces, showing the whites of the eyes and the tongue. At the beginning, haka were performed by warriors before a battle to express strength and intimidate the enemy.

When are haka performed?

Nowadays haka are performed for several reasons: to honour guests, to show the importance of a special occasion or family event – e. g. a birthday, wedding or funeral – and to mark great achievements. The dances express courage, joy or other feelings relevant to the occasion. In recent years many New Zealand sports teams have begun performing haka before international matches and competitions, making the tradition more widely known around the world. The New Zealand rugby team, the All Blacks, have done this since 1905 as a way of challenging their opponents. Anyone who has seen it will probably agree that it's a scary sight!

The cultural effect of haka

Just before the 2011 Rugby World Cup, haka flashmobs were used to show support for the All Blacks. One was famously performed at Trafalgar Square in London, a city with a large New Zealander immigrant community. Other legendary haka that went viral include one performed by New Zealand soldiers in 2012 to honour their comrades who had been killed in Afghanistan, and one performed by hundreds of students at the funeral of a schoolteacher in Palmerston, which attracted over six million online views in a month. Meanwhile, a wedding haka video from January 2016 was viewed over 19 million times. And a haka in Auckland in September 2016 was shared far and wide via social media, attracting more than 20 million views: the video shows more than 160 New Zealand firefighters performing an emotional haka in memory of their colleagues who were killed at the World Trade Center on 9/11. While social media has mainly been responsible for making the haka better known around the globe in the last couple of years, so too have American football teams such as The University of Hawaii Rainbow Warriors, who have made haka part of their pre-game activities.

b) What do the underlined words mean? Write the translations in your exercise book.

Check: Reading

a) Vergleiche deine Antworten mit den Lösungen auf Seite 88 im Workbook.
b) Schätze deine Antworten mit einem grünen oder roten Gesicht ein.

	☺	☹	
1 Konntest du in Aufgabe 3 *skimmen* und dadurch den richtigen Text finden?	○	○	→ 1
2 Konntest du in Aufgabe 3 *scannen* und dadurch in b) schnell die richtigen Antworten finden?	○	○	→ 3a–b
3 Konntest du in Aufgabe 4 wichtige *keywords/phrases* im Text erkennen und markieren?	○	○	→ 3b
4 Konntest du in Aufgabe 4 mit Hilfe deiner *keywords* die Fragen richtig beantworten?	○	○	→ 3b
5 Konntest du in 4b) die Wörter leicht erschließen oder im Wörterbuch schnell finden?	○	○	→ 2

c) Wenn du dich rot eingeschätzt hast, schau dir die rechte Spalte an.
Die Nummern führen dich zu den passenden Übungen im Skills Training (S. 28–29).
Dort kannst du gezielt Reading trainieren.

1 Bringing people together → SF 1–2 (p. 64)

Skim the texts. What is the blog about? Circle A, B or C.

A Charity events

B Organizations that support the homeless

C Winter traditions

TIP:
1 You **skim** to find out the **main information** in a text, not details. What does the whole text tell you about?
2 You **scan** to find **details** in parts of the text with the help of **keywords**.

www. …

Connie's Christmas Charity Dinner was established in 2007 by John Moran and named after his mum, Connie, who adored Christmas. The dinner on 25 December is for homeless people, elderly people who would otherwise spend Christmas alone, refugees and young people who act as carers for their parents and deserve a break. The organizers have spread a little Christmas cheer to thousands of people in need, thanks to generous donations and wonderful volunteers.

The Mega Sleepout takes place during the winter months to raise money for homeless charities. People are sponsored by friends and family. Maya Wilkins, who took part in a sleepout last month, said "Spending a freezing-cold night outside wasn't fun, but I knew I was safe, and I knew I had a choice. Homeless people don't have that luxury. The experience made me realize what a serious issue homelessness is. This is an initiative that really brings people together."

Many organizations have embraced the tradition of **Boxing Day swimming**. On 26 December, huge numbers of swimmers brave freezing temperatures to take a dip in the sea or local lakes or rivers, raising money for the homeless, refugees and ill children. Participants usually forego traditional swimming costumes, instead wearing anything from penguin costumes to Christmas turkey outfits!

The Big Burger Challenge is a burger-eating contest organized every December by Jeremy Griffiths. Contestants try to eat giant four-pound beef patties – the equivalent of 16 normal burgers! Jeremy first ran the event in 2012: 89 people took part and only two managed to eat their burgers – it took the winner an hour to finish. Participants collect money from sponsors, and all the money raised goes to a local mental health charity.

2 What do the words mean? → SF 29 (p. 74)

Find the correct German meaning of these words from exercise 1. Mark the words in the text. Use an English-German dictionary only if necessary.

TIP: Before you use a dictionary:
- Look at the **context**.
- Is there a **similar German** word?
- Do you know a **similar English**, French or Latin word? Or one from another language?
- Look for clues in the **pictures**.

If you need a dictionary, read **all the meanings** of the word and choose the one that fits the context.

1 adore: ______

2 elderly: ______

3 deserve: ______

4 cheer: ______

5 sponsor: ______

6 luxury: ______

7 embrace: ______

8 dip: ______

9 forego: ______

10 contestant: ______

11 beef patties: ______

12 equivalent: ______

3 A useful service ➔ SF 1–2 (p. 64)

a) First read the questions in b). Then scan the text for the answers.

TIP: Mark **keywords** in the questions and look for them or for similar words when you scan. Then read around the keywords to find the answers. Look at the example.
1 If you can't find a keyword, look for a different word or phrase with the same meaning, e. g. 'establish' is the same as 'start'.
2 If the question asks for statistics, look for numbers and also the per cent sign (%).
3 Remember that a verb may be in a different tense in the text: e.g. 'use' in the question may be 'using' in the text.

Teenline Christchurch

Teenline Christchurch supports young people who need practical advice or just someone they can talk to about their problems. It's a free service with professional advisors available to help anyone under 19 in Christchurch. The charity was started in 1996 by Julia Davies, a doctor who noticed that her teenage patients felt awkward talking to their parents or teachers about their problems. She had heard about helplines in other countries and decided to start her own local service.

How it works

Teens can talk to Teenline on the phone and, since 2015, by email or through one-to-one chat with an advisor. "With more and more kids preferring to communicate online, we realized we had to move with the times," explains Dr Davies. "And email and chat can be more private than a telephone call, because nobody can hear what you're saying. Our statistics show that 45 % of kids prefer online chat or email. But 55 % of them still like to speak directly to an advisor. Often a calm, friendly voice is all our callers need." Sometimes, however, kids using the service need more help than Teenline can offer. "Our statistics show that 15 % of these teens have serious issues and must contact their doctor, the police or other organizations to get more support. We help them to do this."

Common issues

Most young people who contact Teenline have relationship issues, says Dr Davies, such as divorce or death in the family, or conflict with parents, brothers and sisters or friends. "The teenage years are a time when people grow and change a lot, and sometimes their friends grow in different directions and this causes conflict," Dr Davies explains. "Bullying is another big topic. And, of course, we get many calls and emails from heartbroken teenagers who have been seeing someone who has treated them badly or broken up with them. We encourage these kids to talk, because it's really important not to keep these feelings inside."

In recent years, Dr Davies has noticed that more and more teens are worried about politics. She doesn't believe that the world has become a more dangerous place for young people, but puts the blame on the internet and social media. "Today all the online media reports about negative events are impossible to miss, and most media don't report the many good things that happen in society. It's no surprise that young people are frightened about issues like pollution and terrorist attacks. Luckily, our advisors can help them to see things from a different perspective, which really helps."

b) Answer the questions.

1 When did Dr Davies establish Teenline Christchurch? ______

2 Do most kids prefer online or telephone contact? ______

3 What percentage of teens who use the service need help from other organizations? ______

4 What kind of relationship problems do young people who use the service have? Name three. ______

______

5 Does Dr Davies think that there are more dangers for today's teens? ______

6 How does Teenline support young people who are worried about the environment? ______

______

c) Summarize the text in your exercise book.

Big dreams – small steps

1 Goals ➔ *SB (p. 56–57)*

Great oaks[1] from little acorns[2] grow.

a) ○ Read pp. 56–57 of your student's book again.
Explain the meaning of this popular saying in your own words.

I think the saying means that

b) Which of the following quotes relates[3] best to the title of this unit? Say why you think so in a few sentences.
You may choose more than one quote. Write in your exercise book.

1 You have to believe in yourself when no one else does – that makes you a winner right there.
Venus Williams

2 Our greatest weakness[4] lies in giving up. The most certain way to succeed[5] is always to try just one more time.
Thomas A. Edison

3 Great things are not done by impulse, but by a series of small things brought together.
Vincent van Gogh

4 It's fine to celebrate success but it is more important to heed[6] the lessons of failure.
Bill Gates

5 The journey of a thousand miles begins with one step.
Lao Tzu

6 It always seems impossible until it's done.
Nelson Mandela

I think quote ... relates best to the title of this unit. It says that ... In other words, ...

c) Find information about the people in b) on the internet. Can you see a connection between the quote and the author's life experience? Explain your point of view.

2 Choosing a direction ➔ *SB (p. 57)*

● Prepare a two-minute talk on the following questions.
Add more ideas in your exercise book first. Then record your talk on a computer, smartphone, etc. If you like, you can play your talk in class.

TIP: In your talk, present your point of view, explain it and give examples.

What goals do young people often have?	Why is it sometimes difficult to achieve these goals?	What positive qualities do you need to achieve an important goal in life? Think about people who achieved their goals.
– study at university – live in another country – bring up a child – earn a lot of money – become famous – …	– not enough time/money/motivation/support – afraid of failing – pressure from outside – friendships and social life	– self-confident/determined – patient – full of energy – believe in yourself – never give up – …

[1]oak [əʊk] *Eiche* [2]acorn ['eɪkɔːn] *Eichel* [3]relate [rɪ'leɪt] *sich beziehen auf* [4]weakness ['wiːknəs] *Schwäche*
[5]succeed [sək'siːd] *erfolgreich sein* [6]heed [hiːd] *beachten*

3 Josh and JB ➜ *SB (pp. 58–60) • SF 3–5 (pp. 64–66) • Wordbank 4*

a) Read pp. 58–60 in your student's book again. Choose one of the five excerpts from *The Crossover* and write it from JB's perspective or from the perspective of Josh's mother (excerpt *Bad News*) in your exercise book.

b) What are Josh's and JB's goals and dreams? Explain how Josh and JB try to achieve these goals. Write in your exercise book.

4 ACCESS TO WORDS Prefixes and suffixes ➜ *SB (p. 61) • GF 1.5 (pp. 77–78)*

a) Write the missing words in the table with a prefix and a suffix, as in the example. Use a dictionary and/or the internet to find the words you don't know.

Adjective (negative)	Adjective (positive)	Noun (positive)
unfriendly	friendly	*friendliness*
	honest	
	intelligent	
	kind	
	patient	
	polite	
	responsible	
	tidy	
	tolerant	

b) How would you describe yourself? How would your family describe you? Write two paragraphs in your exercise book, using at least three words from a). Give reasons. Illustrate them by using examples.

5 REVISION Choices after school (Predictions with *will* and *might*) ➜ *SB (p. 62) • GF 1.5 (pp. 77–78)*

O You have choices. Use I think/I'm (fairly) sure I (probably) will/won't … and I might (not) … to write about your plans after school. Give reasons for your choices.

1 do job training / spend a year abroad / go to university

2 apply for a job in Germany / apply for a job in an English-speaking country

3 do volunteer work abroad / join an environmental organization

4 take an interest in local politics / join a political party

I (don't) think I'll spend …, because … But I might …, because …

6 What's going to happen? (Predictions with the *going to*-future) ➜ *SB (p. 62) • GF 1.5 (pp. 77–78)*

Make a prediction or give a warning about what is going to happen in the following situations. You can use I'm sure …, It looks like … if it fits the situation.

1 You're at a football match with a friend. It's 3–1 for your team in the second half. You say:

It looks like our team is going to win.

2 The sky looks very dark. You and your friend are in the park. You don't have an umbrella. You say:

3 Your sister wants to go to town. The bus leaves in five minutes and she's still at home. You say:

4 You have forgotten to buy your best friend a present for his/her birthday. You think:

5 Your brother has an important test tomorrow, but he hasn't done any work. You say:

6 You have tickets for the cinema, but your friend hasn't arrived yet. While you're waiting you think:

7 EXTRA BACKGROUND FILE College sport in the US ➜ *SB (p. 63) • GF 1 (p. 64)*

Read p. 63 in your student's book again. Answer the questions in a few sentences each.

1 Why can a sport scholarship[1] be important for high school students in the US?

2 Why does Wes have a good chance of getting a sport scholarship?

3 Why is college sport in the US 'big business'?

4 What is Wes hoping for?

[1] scholarship ['skɒləʃɪp] *Stipendium*

8 How to succeed ➜ SB (p. 64) • SF 1–3 (pp. 64–65)

a) Read p. 64 in your student's book again. How does Olivia's story relate to the following quote? Write a short text.

A winner is not someone who never fails. It's someone who never gives up.

b) Describe a situation in which you had to deal with[1] challenges. Explain what you did to succeed. Write in your exercise book.

c) ● What are your next goals in school/sports/private life/your hobby? In three paragraphs, say how you think you might achieve them. Write in your exercise book.

My next goal is to do well in my school exams[2] because …

9 I'll go (Spontaneous decisions: *will*-future) ➜ SB (p. 66) • GF 1.5 (pp. 77)

○ What would you say in the following situations? Make a spontaneous decision with I'll or I won't and a verb from the box.

close · ~~go~~ · lend · lose · pay · tell

1 You're at home and everybody is busy. Someone rings the doorbell.

Oh, there's someone at the door. I'll go. / I'll see who it is.

2 It's cold in the kitchen. The window is open.

3 A friend tells you something that has to stay secret[3].

4 You're in a café with a cousin. She has forgotten her money.

5 A friend needs to make a call, but his phone is at home.

6 You're on a beach with your sister. She wants to go swimming, so she gives you her ring and asks you to keep it safe.

[1] deal with sth. [diːl] *mit etwas umgehen* [2] exam [ɪɡˈzæm] *Prüfung* [3] secret [ˈsiːkrət] *geheim*

10 Planning a meeting (Spontaneous *will* or *going to*) ➜ SB (p. 66) • GF 1.5

Complete the dialogue with *will/won't* or the *going to*-future.

B: I'm going to do my project about climate change in Alaska soon.

A: Oh, I ______ help you. I've just done a project on a similar topic, so I know quite a lot about it. I ______ show it to you if you like.

B: Really? Great! Well, what about Monday after school?

A: No, not Monday. I ______ meet a friend. We ______ look at new computer games. But Tuesday after judo would be OK. I ______ call you when I get home. I ______ forget.

11 A phone call (Spontaneous *will* or *present progressive*) ➜ SB (p. 67) • GF 1.5 (pp. 77)

Complete the dialogue with *will/won't* or with the *present progressive* of a suitable[1] verb.

A: Our basketball team isn't playing/training tomorrow. Let's go skateboarding instead!

B: Sorry, I can't. I ______ my dad tomorrow morning. Then my cousin Frank ______ at lunchtime. He ______ with us for a few days. We ______ to the match in the afternoon.

A: What time? I ______ with you. I ______ anything special. But what if it rains?

B: We ______. We ______ a DVD at home. Oh, wait, there's someone at the door. I ______ stop. I ______ you back. OK?

12 A music competition ➜ SB (p. 67) • SF 12–15 (pp. 69–70)

You are interested in music competitions for young people and you have found information on the internet. Tell an English cousin what you have found. Answer the questions in your exercise book.

Jugend musiziert – seit 1964

- in ganz Deutschland, Wettbewerbe (Instrumente u. Gesang) finden auf 3 Ebenen statt: Regional- ca. 20 000 Teiln. > Landes- (ca. 1/3 davon) > Bundesfinale (über 2000 Teiln.)
- Alter bis 21 J., Wettbewerbe finden meist in (Musik-)Schulen statt.
- Anmeldeformular auf Website ausfüllen (bis November), mit Post an Regionalstelle senden
- selbstausgewählte Stücke (Vorspielzeit bis zu 20 Min.), besser leicht als zu schwer, vom Blatt oder auswendig (keine Punkte extra für auswendig!), Programm muss genehmigt werden.
- Kategorien (Pop u. Klassik, Solo- u. Ensemble): Klavier, Geige, Harfe, Schlagzeug, Gitarre (Pop), Blockflöte, Orgel u. a. Kleinere Instrumente nimmt man selbst mit, große werden gestellt.
- auch Kategorie „neue Musik" (selbstkomponiert!)
- kleine Geld- u. Sachpreise (z. B. Bücher), Wettbewerbe sind öffentlich, kosten nichts.

1 If you want to take part, what do you have to do first?
2 Who can take part?
3 How does the competition work?
4 Who tells you what to play?
5 Do you have to play by heart[2] or can you use music[3]?
6 Can family and friends go to listen?
7 What can you win?
8 About how many students take part? Between 28 and 29 th

First you have to fill in a form that ...

[1]suitable ['su:təbl] *geeignet, passend* [2]by heart [baɪ 'hɑ:t] *auswendig* [3]music *Noten*

13 EXTRA What are they having done? (have something done) ➜ SB (p. 67)

a) Describe what the people are having done.

1

3
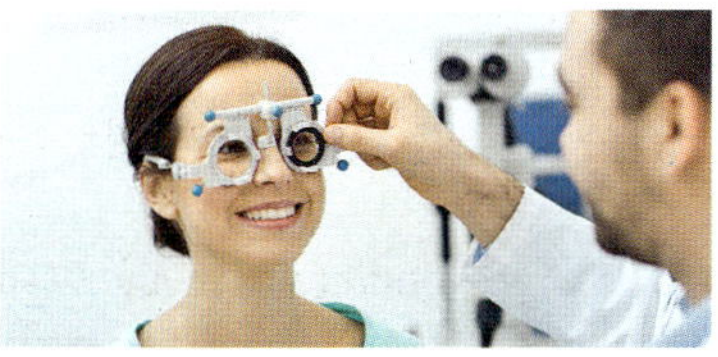

5

2

4
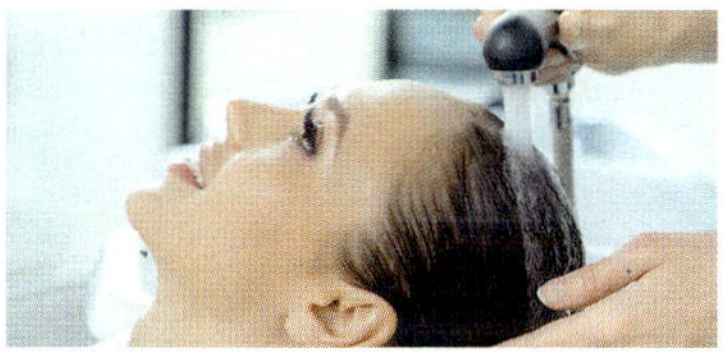

6

1 He*'s/is having his hair cut.* ______

2 They ______ their house ______.

3 ______ her eyes ______.

4 ______.

5 ______.

6 ______.

b) Name four things that you, your family or friends sometimes have done. Write in your exercise book.
We sometimes have our car washed.

14 Writing a good CV ➜ SB (p. 71)

a) Which is the usual order for your personal details at the top of your CV? Write 1–5 in the boxes.
Which personal detail is not usual on a CV? Write ✗ in the box.

☐ Mobile number ☐ Telephone number ☐ Postal address

☐ Name ☐ Date of birth ☐ Email address

b) In which order would you give the following information on your CV? Write 1–5 in the boxes.

☐ Education ☐ Personal statement ☐ Work experience

☐ Hobbies and interests ☐ Qualifications/Skills

c) Anna Kröger would like to spend six weeks working in the UK. She is going to apply for a summer job as a part-time receptionist at a London hotel. Use the information about Anna to write her CV in the correct format, as in your student's book on p. 71.

Tel. +49 (0) 69 95213598, Mobile +49 (0)176 23271945,
lives at Gärtnerstr. 32, 60322 Frankfurt am Main, Germany; Email: ankroeger@gmx.de

Anna was at primary school in Frankfurt from 2006 to 2010. She has been at the Lessing Gymnasium in Frankfurt since 2010. She has a good level of English (six years) and French (four years). She works well with MS Office and photo editing software. She is outgoing and enjoys meeting people, is hard-working and responsible, can organize, likes helping and solving problems and has excellent communication skills. Her parents have a restaurant where she helps at weekends, in the office, as waitress or on the telephone. She has successfully completed a course in basic office management at evening school. She is also interested in volunteer work for environmental projects in the area. Last year she was involved with a local river clean-up. She likes swimming and basketball and plays the keyboard in a local band.

15 Writing a formal letter ➜ *SB (p. 72) • SF 10 (p. 68)*

a) Anna Kröger has to write a letter of application to go with her CV.
Which statements are right (✓) and which are wrong (✗) when you write a formal letter?

- Write your postal address at the top on the right. ◯
- It's better to write 'oe', 'ae', 'ue' and 'ss' instead of 'ö', 'ä', 'ü' and 'ß' in names, e.g. 'Heinrich-Boell-Strasse'. ◯
- You can shorten the date, for example '3.5.17' instead of '3rd May 2017'. ◯
- Use 'Dear Sir or Madam' if you don't know the person you are writing to. ◯
- The first word of the first paragraph starts with a capital letter – different from German. ◯
- You can use short forms (I'll, I've, etc.). ◯
- You can use 'ad' instead of 'advert' or 'advertisement'. ◯
- You shouldn't use informal language like 'great' or 'cool'. ◯

b) ● Write Anna's letter of application for the job of a part-time receptionist to the manager of the Charles Hotel, 20 Coventry Street, London W1D 7AD. For help, look at exercise 1 on p. 72 of your student's book again. Use the space below for notes on layout, then write the letter on the computer.

My address

The Manager

The Charles Hotel

...

16 WORDS Applying for a job ➔ SB (p. 72)

Complete the text with words from the box in the correct form.

advert · achievement · appearance · *application* · apply · candidate · carefully · company · competitive · CV · deadline · experience · goal · include · qualification · self-confident · statement · such as · talkative

Whatever you decide to do after school, you will need a letter of *application* and a good ____________, in English if you ____________ to an international ____________ or organization. There is often a ____________, so read the ____________ ____________ and don't miss the closing date. Your CV must ____________ a short personal ____________ which tells an employer[1] who you are, what you can offer and what your future ____________ are. Furthermore, ____________ and skills, ____________ languages and IT skills, and information about work ____________ you have had are important. If you are an interesting ____________, you may be invited to an interview. Think about your ____________, because clothes, hair and make-up can make a difference. When you answer questions be ____________, but not too ____________. Interviewers don't like applicants who talk too much. Show that you are ____________, but always tell the truth about your ____________. Do your best. Good luck!

17 The same or similar? ➔ SB (p. 73)

a) ○ Write the English words for the following German words. Underline the spelling differences. Can you pronounce the English words correctly? Check with the dictionary (pp. 204–236) in your student's book.

German	English	German	English
Akzent	*accent*	kreativ	
Charakter		kritisieren	
Dialog		kulturell	
filmen		Patient	
global		pessimistisch	
informell		positiv	
intelligent		privat	
Kandidat		relevant	
Kommunikation		respektvoll	

b) Find four more pairs of words that are spelled the same or similarly in German and English. Write a sentence with each English word.

optimistisch – optimistic: You have to be optimistic before an interview, or you won't do well.

[1] employer [ɪm'plɔɪə] *Arbeitgeber*

18 Same sound, different word (Words that sound the same) ➜ SB (p. 73)

a) ● Find a word that sounds the same as words 1–8.

1 aloud ______	3 past ______	5 sauce ______	7 waste ______
2 dear ______	4 principle ______	6 story ______	8 write ______

b) Choose the correct word from a) in the correct form to complete the sentences.

1 Josh and JB's mother is the vice-______ of their school.

2 Will Josh be ______ to go to Duke University? Is he the ______ candidate?

3 When you quote from the internet or a book, you should name your ______.

4 On our camping holiday, we saw lots of ______ in the forest. In the evenings, we sat round the campfire and told funny or scary ______.

c) ● In your exercise book, write three more pairs of words that sound the same.

19 An appointment ➜ SB (p. 73) • SF 22 (p. 71)

a) ○ 17 David Fyodorovych has also applied for the job of a part-time receptionist at the Charles Hotel in London. He calls the hotel. Listen carefully.
What is the reason for David's telephone call? (Circle) A, B or C.

A to change his appointment **B** to make an appointment **C** to check the time of his appointment

b) 17 Listen again. Take notes, then answer questions 1–5 in a few sentences each.

1 Who does David want to speak to and why? ______

2 Who is Nicola? How does she help David? ______

3 Why does Nicola ask David to spell his family name? ______

4 On what day and date will David's interview take place? At what time? ______

5 What else does David ask Nicola? ______

c) 18 Imagine you are David. Listen to Nicola again and, in the pauses, answer her questions in your own words but in a similar way.

20 SPEAKING COURSE Preparing for a job interview ➜ SB (p. 74)

a) Imagine that you want to apply for the job of a part-time receptionist at a hotel in London. The interviewer will probably ask questions like 1–6 below. Prepare good answers to the questions. Think carefully and make notes first.

1 Tell me about yourself. Why are you applying for this job? *like meeting people, ...*

2 Have you worked at a hotel reception before? *No, I haven't but ...*

3 How would you describe a good receptionist? *He/She should ...*

4 Why should we choose you for the job?

5 Are you prepared to work on Saturdays, possibly some evenings too?

6 Tell me more about your language skills. Which languages do you speak, and how well?

b) 19 Now listen to the interviewer's questions and answer them from your notes.

21 Interview tips ➜ SB (p. 74)

A British friend would like to do a summer job in a tourist information office in London. She has been invited to an interview. Give her at least eight good tips before the interview.

Ideas: arrival, appearance, eye contact/body language, personal qualities, possible questions

1 *Don't arrive late, and don't sit down before the interviewer offers you a seat. That's impolite.*

2

3

4

5

6

7

8

1 WORDS Describing character

a) Find the missing adjective.

1 Someone who always tells the truth is an ________________ person.

2 Someone who tries very hard to win or be better than others is ________________.

3 If you are the opposite of lazy, you are ________________.

4 Someone who stays strong in difficult situations or in the face of problems is ________________.

5 At an interview, even if you're nervous, you have to show that you are ________________.

b) Add a prefix to these adjectives to make the opposites:

1 responsible	________	4 polite	________	7 kind	________
2 honest	________	5 patient	________	8 regular	________
3 tolerant	________	6 emotional	________	9 respectful	________

2 What's going to happen? (Predictions with *going to*)

Write sentences in your exercise book. What's going to happen in the pictures? What are they going to do?

1 

2 

3 

The plane ...

3 What are you going to do in the holidays? (*will* or *going to*?)

Complete the sentences and use will/won't or the *going to*-future.

1 In the holidays I ________________ … but I ________________ …

2 Maybe I ________________ … but I ________________ …

3 I'm sure I ________________ …

4 How to write a formal letter

Complete the text with words and phrases that are correct for formal letters.

Write your ________ at the top ________. Begin with '________', if you don't know any names. If you know a name, begin with '________'. You shouldn't use ________ forms (e.g. *I'm*) or informal language, like *great*. In the ________ after the main body, remember to thank the person or organization for considering your application. Finish your letter with 'Yours faithfully' or '________'.

5 Applying for a UK job

a) You want to apply for the job in the advertisement.
First, make notes about the job in the space below.

UK VOLUNTEER WORK PLACEMENT: SUMMER CAMP

We are a youth development charity looking for competent, responsible assistants as support for our summer camp group leaders. Applicants should be able to work well with children (8–12), be creative, reliable and able to keep discipline within the groups. As many of our group activities are outdoors, you will need to be physically fit, a sports person with a love of water sports, climbing and team sports. You should be fluent in English. Previous work experience in this sector would be an advantage.

We provide good quality accommodation in selected host families.
If you are free for 4–6 weeks (July to August) and you think this job is right for you, please contact Fiona Bridges for more details.

b) Write your letter of application on the computer. In the main body of your letter, include information about:

- why you are writing
- your qualifications
- why you would like the job and why you think you could do it well

Check: Writing

a) Vergleiche deine Antworten mit den Lösungen auf Seite 88 im Workbook.
b) Schätze deine Antworten mit einem grünen oder roten Gesicht ein.

	☺	☹	
1 Hast du in Aufgabe 1 verschiedene Adjektive gewusst, die dir helfen, ein *personal statement* zu verfassen und angemessen auf die Interview-Frage 'Tell me about yourself' zu antworten?	○	○	→ 1
2 Hast du in Aufgabe 3 *will* und *going to* richtig eingesetzt? Kannst du sie in einem Gespräch über deine Pläne und Entscheidungen richtig anwenden?	○	○	→ 2
3 Hast du in Aufgabe 4 gewusst, wie man einen formellen Brief schreibt?	○	○	→ 3
4 Hast du in Aufgabe 5b) den Brief im korrekten Layout, Format und Stil schreiben können?	○	○	→ 3, 4

c) Wenn du dich rot eingeschätzt hast, schau dir die rechte Spalte an.
Die Nummern führen dich zu den passenden Übungen im Skills Training (S. 42–43).
Dort kannst du gezielt Writing trainieren.

1 Using adjectives

a) Choose adjectives from the box which describe a person's positive and negative character.

competitive · creative · dishonest · easy-going · friendly · hard-working · helpful · impatient · impolite · intolerant · lazy · mean · practical · relaxed · responsible · rude · self-confident · untidy

1 a positive character: ______________________

____

____

2 a negative character: ______________________

____

____

TIP: When describing yourself it's often good to use adverbs before adjectives, for example *quite, not very, (not) usually, mostly,* etc.
I'm quite hard-working and usually competitive.
To avoid sounding arrogant, begin with, for example, *My friends/People say …* or *I always try to be …*
People say I'm polite and I always try to be helpful.

b) Write a short positive character description of yourself. It should be serious and truthful, but must not sound arrogant. Use adjectives from a) and the advice in the TIP-box.

____

____

____

____

2 Plans and decisions (*will/won't* or *going to*) ➜ GF 1.5 (pp. 77–78)

David and his girlfriend Jessica are talking about jobs and interviews. Complete the sentences with *will/won't* or the correct form of *be going to*.

TIP: Remember:
Use *will* or *won't* for spontaneous decisions. Use *going to* for plans and decisions that somebody has already made.

1 **Jessica:** What ______________ do about the job interview at the hotel?

2 **David:** I ______________ prepare for it as well as I can.

3 **Jessica:** Good idea! I ______________ help you. What if they don't take you?

4 **David:** No problem. I ______________ give up because I need the work experience.
I ______________ look for another job, maybe as a volunteer.

5 **Jessica:** I ______________ apply to a summer camp on the south coast.
I ______________ show you the advert if you like.

6 **David:** A summer camp. Cool! Yes, show it to me, please.
I think I ______________ apply there too!

3 Get it right! ➜ *SF 10 (p. 68)*

Correct the mistakes. Rewrite 1–7 making necessary changes in style, vocabulary, spelling or content.

1 23. Oct., 2017 ______

2 Your ad ______

3 Hello, Mrs Peters, ______

4 Bye, Yours, Maria Fox ______

5 I'm writing about the hotel job. ______

______

6 I am a clever person and a very quick learner. ______

______

7 Please let me know next week if you're going to give me this job. ______

______

4 A work placement at a zoo ➜ *SF 10 (p. 68)* • *Wordbank 5*

Imagine that your 17-year-old cousin Florian would like a volunteer work experience placement in a British zoo. He loves animals and is thinking about becoming a vet[1]. Put together a correct letter of application from the parts in the list. Write the number in the correct place in the letter below.

☐ ☐ ☐ ☐ ☐ ☐ ☐ ☐ ☐ ☐

1 Yours sincerely
2 With best wishes
3 2nd May 20…
4 Thank you for considering my application. I am looking forward to hearing from you.
5 I have had two volunteer work placements of 6 weeks each at Munich Zoo and Nuremberg Zoo.
6 I am writing to apply for the volunteer work placement of keeper support, as advertised on your website.
7 Dear Sir or Madam
8 I would enjoy working as part of a team in animal care and conservation.
9 I hope you like my CV.
10 Chester Zoo
Upton by Chester
Chester CH2 1LH
United Kingdom
11 Blumenstr. 28
85049 Ingolstadt
Germany
12 Your advert

[1] vet [vet] *Tierarzt*

4 Unit

Connect through English

1 A year abroad ➔ *SB (pp. 76–77)*

a) Read pp. 76–77 of your student's book again. Think about the advantages and disadvantages of spending a year abroad while you are still at high school. Make notes in two lists to discuss in class.

For	Against
…	…

b) If you took part in the competition on p. 76, which would be the English-speaking country of your choice? Say why, and discuss your choice in class.

2 English in everyday life ➔ *SB (pp. 76–77)*

a) Think about how much English you see, read, or hear outside school on a typical day. Where do you come across English outside school? Ideas: TV, internet, sports, magazines, adverts, etc. Make notes for a class discussion.

b) Apart from English lessons and homework, how much English do you actively write, read, speak or listen to every day? Ideas: social media, friends who don't speak German, etc. Make notes for a class discussion.

3 An email ➔ *SB (p. 77) • Wordbank 6*

Write an email to a new friend you have met on social media. The friend speaks no German, only his/her own language, but good English. Introduce yourself and give some information:

- how long you have been learning English
- what you find easy/difficult (e. g. spelling, pronunciation, tenses)
- why learning English is important to you
- what you need English for (entertainment, internet, travel, etc.)
- why you will most probably need English after school

Hi!
…
We seem to have similar interests, so maybe …
I've been learning … since I was …
Everybody says English is supposed to be …
However, I find …
From my point of view …
I actually listen to … every day because …
Talking about my …, I'm sure I'll/won't need English …
…

Wordbank 1: Talking about nature – Adjectives

majestic	low	rugged	bare
impressive	high	jagged	snowy
spectacular	tall		snow-covered
	towering		tree-covered
	steep		rocky

TIP: When you use more than one adjective before a noun, **comment adjectives** (e. g. beautiful, unusual) and **size adjectives** (e. g. huge, tall) usually come first and second. Other adjectives follow.
As a guideline, follow the sequence of the columns in the tables on these pages.
It's usually better style to use just two, or at most three, adjectives, e. g. *towering, rocky mountains*.

	beautiful	large	colourful	tropical
	interesting	small	exotic	land
a/an	rare	tall	predatory	sea
	unique	short	wild	

	cute	large	tame	marine
	endangered	huge	dangerous	furry
a/an	extraordinary	small	poisonous	forest
	rare	tiny	deadly	
	unusual		wild	

	amazing	large	ancient	dense
	remarkable	colossal	pristine	green
a/an	spectacular	endless	untouched	lush
	wonderful	vast		tropical

ancient ['eɪnʃənt] *(ur)alt* **at most** *höchstens* **bare** *kahl* **colossal** [kə'lɒsl] **dense** *dicht* **endangered** *gefährdet; vom Aussterben bedroht* **furry** ['fɜːri] *Pelz-* **impressive** *beeindruckend* **jagged** ['dʒægɪd] *zerklüftet* **low** *niedrig* **lush** *üppig* **majestic** [mə'dʒestɪk] *majestätisch, mächtig* **nature** ['neɪtʃə] *Natur* **predatory** ['predətri] *Raub-* **pristine** ['prɪstiːn] *ursprünglich, unberührt* **rare** *selten* **remarkable** *erstaunlich, bemerkenswert* **rugged** ['rʌgɪd] *rau, schroff* **sequence** ['siːkwəns] *Abfolge, Reihenfolge* **spectacular** [spek'tækjələ] **tame** *zahm* **towering** *hoch aufragend* **unique** [ju'niːk] *einzigartig* **untouched** *unberührt* **vast** [vɑːst] *riesig*

Wordbank 1: Talking about nature – Adjectives

a/an	beautiful	long	narrow	shallow	straight	... river
	charming	large	wide	deep	winding	
		short		rough	slow-moving	
				gentle	fast-moving	

a/an	attractive	little	wide	shallow	freshwater	... lake
	lovely	large		deep	saltwater	
	delightful	huge				
		immense				

a/an	beautiful	long	straight	unspoilt	rocky	... coastline
	dramatic	extensive	curving	untouched	rugged	
	striking	steep			wild	
	stunning					

a/an	lovely	long	secluded	unspoilt	sandy	... beach
	incredible	endless	lonely	pristine	golden	
	breathtaking	extensive		deserted	rocky	
				empty		

Make phrases with each of the nouns on these two pages. Use two or three adjectives.

1 *magnificient snow-covered mountains*

2 ______________________

3 ______________________

4 ______________________

5 ______________________

6 ______________________

7 ______________________

8 ______________________

breathtaking *atemberaubend* **charming** *bezaubernd* **curving** *gekrümmt* **delightful** *entzückend, herrlich* **deserted** [dɪˈzɜːtɪd] *menschenleer, einsam* **extensive** [ɪkˈstensɪv] *ausgedehnt, weitläufig* **gentle** *sanft, sacht* **immense** *enorm* **incredible** [ɪnˈkredəbl] *unglaublich, sagenhaft* **secluded** [sɪˈkluːdɪd] *abgeschieden, einsam* **shallow** *flach, seicht* **striking** *auffallend, beeindruckend* **unspoilt** [ˌʌnˈspɔɪlt] *unberührt, unverbaut* **winding** [ˈwaɪndɪŋ] *gewunden, kurvenreich*

 Fotos: **Fotolia** (beach: Rafael Ben-Ari/Chameleons Eye; coastline: jovannig; lake: norinori303); **Shutterstock** (river: AustralianCamera)

Talking about novels

Plot

The story/novel/play/poem/… is about/deals with …
The overall theme/**message** is …
The title refers to …
In the course of the story we see that …
As the story **unfolds**, we learn that …
The author creates | **tension** | by describing …
| **suspense** | by using | words that …
| the image of …
There is a **turning point/surprising twist** when …
The story has an **open ending**, so …

Setting

The story is set in ...
The story takes place during/in …
The setting creates | tension/suspense.
| a dark/mysterious/tense/… **mood**.
The setting contributes to | the romantic/comical/adventurous/… **atmosphere**.
| the significance of …

Character

The main character/**hero**/**protagonist** is …
… is a likable/shady/ruthless/odd/… character.
He/She **comes across** as a strong/weak/aggressive/brave/funny/serious … person.
The way … speaks/behaves/dresses/… tells us that …
In the course of the story, | the character faces …
| (Julie) **undergoes a change** when …
He/She **revealed** his/her true character when …
There is a decisive moment for … when …
The **relationship** between the characters is influenced by …

Perspective

The story is told by a **first-person/third-person narrator**.
The narrator is (not) a character in the story.
He/She tells the story in a funny/serious/**ironic**/exciting/**thrilling**/… way.
As a first-person narrator he/she | has only a **limited point of view**.
| tells the story in a personal/emotional/… way.
The perspective is one-sided.
We feel as if we enter the mind of …

adventurous [əd'ventʃərəs] *abenteuerlich* **aggressive** [ə'gresɪv] *aggressiv* **come across** *auf andere wirken, rüberkommen* **comical** ['kɒmɪkl] *komisch, witzig* **contribute to** [kən'trɪbjuːt tə] *zu etwas beitragen* **deal with** *handeln von* **decisive** [dɪ'saɪsɪv] *entscheidend* **face** *begegnen* **influence** ['ɪnfluəns] *beeinflussen* **in the course** *im Verlauf* **ironic** [aɪ'rɒnɪk] *ironisch* **likable** ['laɪkəbl] *nett, liebenswert* **limited** ['lɪmɪtɪd] *limitiert* **mysterious** [mɪ'stɪəriəs] *mysteriös, geheimnisvoll* **narrator** [nə'reɪtə(r)] *Erzähler* **odd** [ɒd] *eigenartig* **one-sided** *einseitig* **overall** [ˌəʊvər'ɔːl] *übergreifend* **plot** [plɒt] *Handlung* **protagonist** [prə'tægənɪst] *Hauptfigur* **romantic** [rəʊ'mæntɪk] *romantisch* **ruthless** ['ruːθləs] *rücksichtslos* **shady** ['ʃeɪdi] *dubios, fragwürdig* **significance** [sɪg'nɪfɪkəns] *Bedeutung* **suspense** [sə'spens] *Spannung* **tense** [tens] *(an)gespannt* **thrilling** ['θrɪlɪŋ] *spannend* **turning point** *Wendepunkt* **twist** [twɪst] *Wendung* **undergo** *durchmachen* **unfold** [ʌn'fəʊld] *entfalten, offenlegen* **weak** *schwach*

Wordbank 3: Talking about film

1 Perspective

high angle shot
[ˌhaɪ‿æŋgl ˈʃɒt]
Aufnahme aus der Vogelperspektive

low angle shot
[ˌləʊ‿æŋgl ˈʃɒt]
Aufnahme aus der Froschperspektive

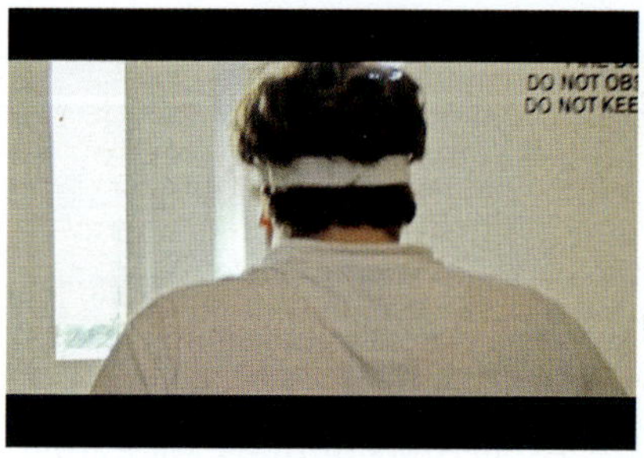

over-the-shoulder shot
[ˌəʊvə ðə ˈʃəʊldə ʃɒt]
Aufnahme „über die Schulter"

2 Camera

close-up
[ˈkləʊs ʌp]
Nahaufnahme

long shot
[ˌlɒŋ ˈʃɒt]
Totale

medium shot
[ˈmiːdiəm ʃɒt]
Halbtotale

3 Making films

cut [kʌt] *Schnitt*	music [ˈmjuːzɪk] *Musik*	scene [siːn] *Szene*	screenplay [ˈskriːnpleɪ] *Drehbuch*	setting [ˈsetɪŋ] *Handlungsort/-zeit*
slow motion [ˌsləʊ ˈməʊʃn] *Zeitlupe*	special effects [ˌspeʃl‿ɪˈfekts] *Spezialeffekte*	split screen [splɪt ˈskriːn] *geteilter Bildschirm*	zoom in [ˌzuːm‿ˈɪn] *reinzoomen*	zoom out [ˌzuːm‿ˈaʊt] *rauszoomen*

4 People

actor/actress [ˈæktə/ˈæktrəs] *Schauspieler/in*	director [dəˈrektə] *Regisseur/in*	producer [prəˈdjuːsə] *Produzent/in*	main character [ˌmeɪn ˈkarəktə] *Hauptfigur*	supporting charcter [səˌpɔːtɪŋˈkærəktə] *Nebenfigur*
editor [ˈedɪtə] *Cutter/in*	composer [kəmˈpəʊzə] *Komponist/in*	audience [ˈɔːdiəns] *Zuschauer/innen*	costume designer [ˈkɒstjuːm dɪˌzaɪnə] *Kostümbildner/in*	film critic [ˈfɪlm ˌkrɪtɪk] *Fimkritiker/in*

5 Genres

documentary [ˌdɒkjuˈmentri] *Dokumentarfilm*	crime story [ˈkraɪm stɔːri] *Krimi*	short film [ˌʃɔːt ˈfɪlm] *Kurzfilm*	advertisement [ədˈvɜːtɪsmənt] *Werbung*	science fiction [ˌsaɪəns ˈfɪkʃn] *Science-Fiction*
animated film [ˌænɪmeɪtɪd ˈfɪlm] *Animationsfilm*	comedy [ˈkɒmədi] *Komödie*	drama [ˈdrɑːmə] *Drama*	love story [ˈlʌv stɔːri] *Liebesfilm*	action film [ˈækʃn fɪlm] *Actionfilm*

 Fotos: Aviary / Corrie Chen / interfilm Berlin Management GmbH

1 Useful adjectives

admired
[əd'maɪəd]
bewundert

alarmed
[ə'lɑːmd]
beunruhigt

amused
[ə'mjuːzd]
vergnügt, belustigt

astonished
[ə'stɒnɪʃt]
erstaunt

blissful
['blɪsfl]
glückselig

concerned
[kən'sɜːnd]
betroffen

confident
['kɒnfɪdənt]
(selbst)sicher

confused
[kən'fjuːzd]
irritiert

content
[kən'tent]
zufrieden

delighted
[dɪ'laɪtɪd]
erfreut

depressed
[dɪ'prest]
deprimiert

disgusted
[dɪs'gʌstɪd]
angewidert

entertained
[ˌentə'teɪnd]
unterhalten

exhausted
[ɪg'zɔːstɪd]
erschöpft

fabulous
['fæbjələs]
fabelhaft

flattered
['flætəd]
geschmeichelt

frustrated
[frʌ'streɪtɪd]
frustriert

furious
['fjʊəriəs]
wütend

gleeful
['gliːfl]
schadenfroh

indifferent
[ɪn'dɪfrənt]
gleichgültig

irritated
['ɪrɪteɪtɪd]
genervt

naughty
['nɔːti]
frech, unartig

upset
[ʌp'set]
gekränkt, benommen

vulnerable
['vʌlnərəbl]
verletzlich

worried
['wʌrid]
besorgt

2 Idiomatic expressions

positive feelings

to look on the bright side
die Dinge positiv sehen
to have your heart in the right place
das Herz am richtigen Fleck haben
to be head over heels in love
Hals über Kopf verliebt sein
to be on top of the world
überglücklich sein
to be on the same wavelength
auf der gleichen Wellenlänge sein

negative feelings

to be bored to tears
sich zu Tode langweilen
to be beside yourself
neben sich stehen
to be down in the dumps
sich niedergeschlagen fühlen
to have a chip on one's shoulder
in reizbarer Stimmung sein
to go up the wall
die Wände hochgehen

Illustrationen: Shutterstock (pingebat)

Wordbank 5: Letter of application

How to start

If you don't know who you are writing to

Dear Sir
Dear Madam
Dear Sir/Madam

If you know who you are writing to

Dear Mr Smith
Dear Mrs Smith
Dear Ms Smith

The first sentence

I am writing to apply for the position/post of ...
I wish to apply for the post of … which you advertised in … on …
I read your advertisement for a … in … with great interest.
I refer to your advertisement in … dated …
I would like to apply for the position of …
As discussed on the phone today I am sending you my personal documentation.
Having completed my training as a/an …,
I am now looking for a post in …

Your education/qualifications

I graduated from … in …
I hold a certificate/degree in …
I have been working as a/an …
I am currently (a student/employed) at …
I have completed the following courses: …
I will graduate this year with … (a Bachelor of Arts)

Giving information about yourself

I am particularly interested in this job, as …
I would like to work for you in order to …
My strengths are …
I am currently attending … (school) where I am doing a course in … (subject).
Currently I am working for … and my responsibilities include …
During … I did an internship abroad.
During my time as …, I improved/extended/ my knowledge of …
Even under pressure I can maintain high standards.
In addition to my responsibilities as …, I also developed … skills.

What skills you have acquired

I have experience of …
As my references show …
I feel I have necessary qualities for this job because …
I am a motivated professional with a variety of skills and experience.
I would also like to add …
I would be well suited to the position because …
During … I have taken a great interest in working (together) with …
This job would give me the opportunity to extend my knowledge of … / to use my IT skills.
I wish to work abroad and make use of my knowledge of languages.
My native language is …, but I can also speak …
I have a working knowledge of …
I am an experienced user of …

How to finish

I can give you the following names as references.
I am available for the interview …
I would be delighted to be invited to an interview.
I look forward to meeting you / hearing from you (soon).
I see new tasks / this position as a welcome challenge, which I look forward to.

If you don't know who you are writing to
Yours faithfully,

If you know who you are writing to
Yours sincerely,

acquire [ə'kwaɪə] *erwerben* **advertise** ['ædvətaɪz] *inserieren* **advertisement** [əd'vɜːtɪsmənt] *Inserat* **Bachelor of Arts** ['bætʃələ] *unterster akademischer Grad* **delight** [dɪ'laɪt] *erfreuen* **employ** [ɪm'plɔɪ] *anstellen* **Yours faithfully** ['feɪθfəli] *Mit freundlichen Grüßen* **graduate** ['grædʒueɪt] *einen (Schul)Abschluss machen* **internship** ['ɪntɜːnʃɪp] *Praktikum* **maintain** [meɪn'teɪn] *aufrechterhalten* **major** ['meɪdʒə] *im Hauptfach studieren* **motivate** ['məʊtɪveɪt] *motivieren* **native language** ['neɪtɪv] *Muttersprache* **particularly** [pə'tɪkjələli] *besonders* **reference** ['refrəns] *Empfehlung* **suited** [suːtɪd] *geeignet* **variety** [və'raɪəti] *Vielzahl*

Describing a language

a **first** / a **native** / an **indigenous** language
a **mother** / a **native** tongue
a **foreign** / a **non-native** / an **unfamiliar** language
a **second** / an **additional** / an **official** language
a **common** / a **shared** language
a **world** / a **global** / a **universal** / an **international** language

Complete sentence 1 and write a second sentence using words from the box above.

1 My native language is ________________, but I speak ______________ as a/an _______________ language.

2 ____

Talking about communication

A language is **a medium / a means / a tool** of communication.
(to) speak English / French / … **fluently / adequately / poorly**
(to) need an **interpreter / a translator / …**
(to) communicate **across languages / across national borders / in a globalized world**
(to) **be fluent in / communicate through / correspond through / negotiate through** English / French / …

Complete these sentences using words or phrases from the two boxes above.

1 If you are fluent in ____

2 If you want to communicate across ____________________________________

How languages are used

English **French** **Latin** …	is/was **used** has been/was **introduced** has been/was **adopted**	for in	**international / official / written** communication. international **correspondence / negotiations**.
		by	**the church/the government / the upper class.** **churchmen / civil servants / diplomats.** **scholars / scientists / explorers.**
	is has become was became	**the language of**	**advertising / business / commerce / trade.** **administration / government / diplomacy.** **aviation / air traffic control / shipping.** **education / research / science / technology / scholarship / religion.**

Write two sentences using the words in brackets and words or phrases from the box above.

1 (the Middle Ages, Latin) ____

2 (English, trade and diplomacy) ______________________________________

additional [ə'dɪʃənl] *zusätzliche(r, s)* adequately ['ædɪkwətli] *ausreichend* administration [ədˌmɪnɪ'streɪʃn] *Verwaltung* adopt *übernehmen, annehmen* advertising ['ædvətaɪzɪŋ] *Werbung* air traffic control *Flugsicherung* civil servant *Beamte(r)* commerce ['kɒmɜːs] *Handel* correspond [ˌkɒrə'spɒnd] *korrespondieren* correspondence *Korrespondenz, Briefwechsel* fluent ['fluːənt] *fließend* indigenous [ɪn'dɪdʒənəs] *einheimisch* interpreter [ɪn'tɜːprɪtə] *Dolmetscher/in* means *Mittel* medium *Medium, Mittel* mother tongue/native tongue [tʌŋ] *Muttersprache* negotiate [nɪ'gəʊʃieɪt] *verhandeln* negotiation [nɪˌgəʊʃi'eɪʃn] *Verhandlung* poorly *schlecht* scholar ['skɒlə] *Gelehrte(r)* scholarship *Wissenschaft* shipping *Schifffahrt* the Middle Ages *das Mittelalter* tool *Werkzeug* universal [ˌjuːnɪ'vɜːsl] *universell* upper class *Oberschicht*

Discussing advantages and disadvantages

Useful adjectives

the **main / primary / major** (dis)advantage
a **definite / serious** (dis)advantage
an **enormous** / a **huge** (dis)advantage
another / a **further /** an **additional** (dis)advantage
a **possible / potential** (dis)advantage
a **slight** (dis)advantage

Listing the pros and cons

\+ **The fact that** (you can cycle there / …) **is a huge / major advantage**.
This **has the (enormous) advantage** that …
The **main benefit** this brings is …
The **upside (of this)** is …
The fact that (hostels are cheap / …) **allows you to** …
This **helps you to** …
(The price / …) **is another positive aspect**.

– However, there are also **a number of disadvantages.**
One **possible / potential drawback** is …
The **downside (of this)** is …
This **makes it difficult / impossible to** …
(The effect on the environment / …) **is another negative aspect.**

Weighing up the arguments

On the one hand … On the other hand …
These advantages make up for …
Despite these (dis)advantages …
We also have to take into account that …*

Drawing a conclusion

On balance,	it seems that …
On the whole,	you can argue that …
All in all,	it is hard to deny that …
All things considered,	**it is safe to say that …**

Having looked at both sides of the argument, …*
The advantages (by far) outweigh the disadvantages.*

Giving your own opinion

In my opinion / view, …
I (personally) believe that …
To me it seems (that) …
As far as I'm concerned, …

*These phrases are rather formal.
They are mainly used in written English.

additional [əˈdɪʃənl] *zusätzliche(r, s)* **all things considered** [kənˈsɪdəd] *alles in allem* **as far as I'm concerned** [kənˈsɜːnd] *was mich betrifft* **aspect** [ˈæspekt] **benefit** [ˈbenɪfɪt] *Vorteil, Nutzen* **by far** *bei weitem* **definite** *deutliche(r, s), entschiedene(r, s)* **despite** [dɪˈspaɪt] *trotz* **draw a conclusion** *schlussfolgern* **drawback** *Nachteil* **enormous** [ɪˈnɔːməs] **major** [ˈmeɪdʒə] *bedeutende(r, s)* **make up for sth.** *etwas ausgleichen* **on balance** [ˈbæləns] *alles in allem* **on the whole** *alles in allem* **outweigh sth.** [ˌaʊtˈweɪ] *schwerer wiegen als etwas* **potential** [pəˈtenʃl] *potentielle(r, s)* **primary** [ˈpraɪməri] *grundlegende(r, s)* **pros and cons** *(pl) Vor- und Nachteile* **rather** [ˈrɑːðə] *ziemlich* **slight** [slaɪt] *klein, leicht* **take sth. into account** *etwas berücksichtigen, beachten* **the upside** *der Vorteil, das Gute* **weigh sth. up** [weɪ] *etwas abwägen*

4 Facts about English
➜ SB (p. 78) • SF 1 (p. 64)

a) Read p. 78 exercise 1 of your student's book again. Think about your answers, then answer the questions below in a few sentences each.

1 When did you use English as a lingua franca? Describe at least two situations.

2 In Sweden and Denmark about 70 percent of the population can speak English. What do you think the reasons are?

3 What motivates people all over the world to learn English? Give three or more reasons.

5 English native speakers and other languages
➜ SB (p. 78) • Wordbank 6

Since English is used as a lingua franca, what effect do you think this fact has on English native speakers learning other languages? Research the language-learning situation in the UK and the USA. Make notes below and report what you find to the class.

6 SPEAKING COURSE The power of pictures ➜ SB (p. 79)

a) Read p. 79 of your student's book again. Then choose photo 1 or 2 and describe it using STEP 1:

- general description
- position of the main elements
- detail about the scene
- stylistic elements

1

2

I have chosen ______________________

b) Now use STEPS 2 and 3 to analyse and comment on your photo.

c) What impression does each photo make on you? Compare the atmosphere. How does each photo make you feel?

7 In bear country

➜ SB (p. 80) • SF 12–15 (pp. 69–70)

You are planning a walking tour in British Columbia, Canada. You meet two backpackers from Poland who speak English but no German. It's their first time in bear country. They ask you some questions about safety. You have a flyer with some information. Use it to answer their questions in English. Don't translate. Report only the important points in your own words.

Was Sie über Bären wissen müssen

Schwarzbären und Grizzlybären sind in Kanada zu Hause. Bären können sehr schnell laufen, sind gute Kletterer und Schwimmer. Sie sehen so gut wie der Mensch, hören aber besser und haben einen hervorragenden Geruchssinn. Es könnte sogar sein, dass Bären den besten Geruchssinn aller Tiere haben. In der Regel geht ein Bär dem Menschen aus dem Weg, es sei denn, er wird überrascht.

Verhaltensregeln

In jedem Nationalpark geben Ranger Auskunft über richtige Verhaltensregeln.

! Wandern Sie nicht allein sondern in kleinen Gruppen von mindestens vier Personen.
! Bleiben Sie in der Gruppe zusammen.
! Wenn ein Bär sich in der Gegend aufhält, darf er nicht überrascht werden. Machen Sie sich also bemerkbar, indem Sie sich laut unterhalten, lachen oder singen.
! Falls Sie in der Ferne einen Bären entdecken, bleiben Sie ruhig und nehmen Sie sofort eine andere Route. Lenken Sie keine Aufmerksamkeit auf sich.
! Nehmen Sie aufgestellte Warnschilder ernst.
! Bleiben Sie auf den empfohlenen Wegen.
! Tragen Sie für alle Fälle eine Dose Bärenabwehrspray mit sich.

Wenn Sie einem Bären begegnen

! Laufen Sie nicht weg. Der Bär kann Sie jederzeit mit Leichtigkeit einholen.
! Geraten Sie nicht in Panik und schreien Sie nicht.
! Der Bär sollte Sie als Mensch und nicht als Beutetier wahrnehmen. Sprechen Sie also mit ruhiger, leiser Stimme und vermeiden Sie Augenkontakt mit dem Tier.
! Gehen Sie nie an ein Tier näher heran, um Fotos zu machen.
! Versuchen Sie nie, ein wildes Tier zu füttern. Das ist strengstens verboten.

Camping

! Zelten Sie nicht in der freien Natur sondern nur auf einem offiziellen Zeltplatz.
! Kochen und essen Sie nicht in der Nähe Ihres Lagerplatzes. Die Entfernung zwischen Zelt und Kochplatz sollte mindestens 50 Meter betragen.
! Nehmen Sie nichts Essbares mit ins Zelt. Ein Bär würde es riechen und suchen.
! Besorgen Sie bärensichere Behälter für Ihre Lebensmittel.
! Halten Sie Ihren Zeltplatz sauber. Essensreste und Abfälle sollten in luftdichten Behältern aufbewahrt werden. Bären lieben Abfälle.

1 Are bears aggressive? We heard that you have to climb a tree if you see one. Is that true?

2 If you see a bear that is still far away, what should you do?

3 If you suddenly see a bear quite close, what should you do? What shouldn't you do?

4 Can we take a tent with us?

5 And what about food?

6 Can bears see, hear and smell like humans?

8 ACCESS TO WORDS Travelling ➜ SB (p. 81)

Ron

a) ○ Complete Ron's text with suitable travel words from p. 81 of your student's book.

I didn't book my holiday at a ________________ . I did it online because it was cheaper: a direct flight with Cathay Pacific for about £600. At the ________________ , I checked in my ________________ , just one large ________________ . My carry-on bag was my old ________________ , which always weighs 7 kilos, the full baggage allowance. I already had my boarding pass on my phone. After that I went straight to ________________ control. Luckily, the officer recognized me as the guy in the photo. There was a long queue at ________________ . I had to take off my trainers and empty my pockets. Then I went to Gate 18 and found a seat in the departure lounge. Somehow I fell asleep and I didn't hear the first ________________ , but I woke up when my phone rang – it was Mum telling me not to go in the sun because I had forgotten my ________________ . On the plane, a ________________ soon served us with snacks and drinks, so I felt better. Our ________________ was about twelve hours, so I had enough time to read every page of my new ________________ . I also read through my tour ________________ . The ________________ would be in small hotels or ________________ , good places for ________________ people and making friends from different ________________ and cultures. I was really looking forward to Hong Kong and China!

b) Read the text again and say what you think the following words and phrases mean.

1 carry-on bag: ________________

2 baggage allowance: ________________

3 boarding pass: ________________

4 departure lounge: ________________

c) Complete the sentences with correct verbs and/or prepositions.

1 What time are you ________________ Heathrow?

2 Are you going ________________ tube?

3 Do you know where to ________________ off?

4 My flight leaves ________________ Terminal 5.

5 Did you have to ________________ a visa for Russia?

6 Are you going to ________________ organized tours?

7 I have to learn the Russian alphabet so I'll know where to ________________ and off the metro.

9 Small problems ➜ *SB (pp. 82–83) • SF 1 (p. 64)*

For people connecting in English, language differences or cultural differences can sometimes cause problems. Read the following texts and identify the problem.
Then explain it in a few sentences.

1

Marie from Germany had just arrived at JFK Airport. It was her first time in the US and she was excited. Someone from her host family was going to collect her from *Arrivals*. She waited, but nobody came. Suddenly someone tapped her on the shoulder from behind, a tall dark guy with a friendly smile. "Hi, you must be Marie from Germany. Right? I'm Josh, the son of the family. Nice to meet you. Come on. This way."

Josh picked up her largest bag but Marie said loudly, "Oh, Josh, you mustn't carry my bag." So Josh put it down again and thought, "How strange. Why doesn't she want me to help her with the bag? What can be in it?" But Josh didn't say anything. As they walked through the airport Marie thought, "Why did he put my bag down again? Was it too heavy for him? Strange guy."

What was the problem? Why didn't Josh and Marie understand each other?

2

Tom was visiting his cousin Nathan in Boston. The boys had a good time sightseeing and meeting friends, and Tom's English was already quite good. On Friday evening, the boys were talking about plans for the weekend. "It's going to be 32 degrees tomorrow, it said on the weather report. I hope you have some warm clothes with you, Tom," said Nathan. Tom didn't answer. How strange! Warm clothes when it's 32 degrees? Maybe Nathan meant clothes for warm weather …

What was the problem?
Why didn't Tom understand?

3

Lena from Essen was in New York with her exchange student Madison. The girls wanted to go shopping at Macy's, the famous department store. At the main doors Madison said, "I just have to go somewhere for Mom first. You go on in and look around. I'll meet you near the elevators on the first floor in about ten minutes. Don't get lost! OK?" Lena didn't get lost. She looked at trendy bags and jewellery, then went to the meeting place on time.

She looked for Madison, but she wasn't there. Where was she? After twenty minutes Lena decided to look for Madison outside. She went down the stairs to the main doors – and suddenly she saw Madison waiting by the elevators. "Hey, there you are!" Lena said. "But you said the first floor! That's where I was!"

Can you explain the situation?

1 WORDS Chat at the airport

Dave and Lena meet in a hostel. Complete the dialogue with words in the correct form.

Dave: Is German your ______________________?

Lena: Yes, it is. I'm from Essen. After school, I'd like to do a ______________________ year to improve my English, maybe in Australia or Canada. If I'm lucky, maybe I'll win a one-year ______________________.

Dave: My German isn't very good, but in Stuttgart I was able to make ______________________. People speak quite fast, so I always had to ask them to ______________________. I've just come back from Australia. The plane was full of ______________________ with rucksacks. All the ______________________ were full. I couldn't even find a ______________________ for my jacket, so the ______________________ had to help me. Would you like to see the ______________________ of my trip? I started out in Sydney and went up the east coast to Cairns.

Lena: Sounds good. How much are small hotels and hostels? Is ______________________ expensive?

Dave: Well, let's go for a coffee and I'll tell you!

2 Travel talk

Complete the text with a verb and correct preposition. Use get, go and leave in the correct tense and form.

We ______________ Verona at 22:15, on the night train. Somebody told us the train ______________ platform 11, but it was platform 15, so we had to run. Luckily, we managed to ______________ the train just before it left. We ______________ a cycle tour of the city. ______________ bike is the best way to see the sights. We could stop and ______________ for a photo stop whenever we wanted. Verona is cool!

3 Cycling in Vancouver

20 At a youth hostel in Vancouver, Max and Lara from Germany meet Zofia from Poland. Max has been on a city cycling tour and he tells Lara about it. Listen and take notes in your exercise book. Then answer Zofia's questions in English. What does Max answer?

1 How many people can be in a group? And was there a guide?
2 What's so special about Stanley Park?
3 What did you learn about Gastown?
4 What other highlights did you see?
5 How much was your tour and what did it include?

4 German youth hostels

You meet some Chinese students who speak English but not German. They want to stay at youth hostels in Germany but they don't know much about them. You find the following information on your phone. Explain the hostel rules to them in English. Tell them what they have to do and what they are not allowed to do 1) on arrival, 2) during their stay and 3) when they leave. Take notes first then present the rules in two minutes to the students.

Hausordnung für Jugendherbergen

Das Deutsche Jugendherbergswerk wünscht allen Gästen einen angenehmen und erlebnisreichen Aufenthalt in seinen Jugendherbergen! […] Die Jugendherbergen haben Hausregeln, die helfen sollen, die unterschiedlichen Bedürfnisse der Gäste zu berücksichtigen und einen spannungsarmen Aufenthalt zu ermöglichen. Die folgenden Grundregeln sollen daher von allen Gästen beachtet werden. Gruppenleiter und Lehrer sind verantwortlich für ihre Gruppen.

Ankunft

Wenn Sie angemeldet sind, können Sie Ihre Ankunftszeit mit der Herbergsleitung vereinbaren. Zugesagte Plätze werden bis 18 Uhr freigehalten, danach können sie an andere Gäste vergeben werden. Wenn Sie nicht angemeldet sind, können Sie telefonisch oder direkt in der Jugendherberge erfahren, ob es freie Plätze gibt. Wer in einer Jugendherberge übernachten oder andere Angebote in Anspruch nehmen möchte, muss Mitglied des Deutschen Jugendherbergswerkes oder eines anderen nationalen Jugendherbergsverbandes sein. Reisende mit deutscher Anschrift ohne Mitgliedskarte können auch in der Jugendherberge Mitglied werden, ausländische Gäste ohne Mitgliedskarte müssen eine „Internationale Gastkarte" erwerben.

Aufenthalt

Die Unterbringung erfolgt in Mehrbettzimmern und in der Regel nach Geschlecht getrennt. Familien können nach Anmeldung in einem Zimmer gemeinsam untergebracht werden, sofern es verfügbar ist. Wir bitten Sie während Ihres Aufenthaltes um Mithilfe. Dazu gehört z. B., dass Sie die von Ihnen genutzten Einrichtungen, Räume und Gegenstände in Ordnung halten und beim Tischdienst helfen.
Die Jugendherbergen haben sich dem Umwelt- und Naturschutz verpflichtet. Darum bitten wir Sie, Abfall getrennt zu sammeln oder ganz zu vermeiden und mit Energie und Wasser sparsam umzugehen.
In Schlafräumen dürfen Speisen weder zubereitet noch gegessen werden. Aus brandschutztechnischen, versicherungs- und gesundheitsrechtlichen Gründen ist die Benutzung von elektrischen Geräten für die Zubereitung von Speisen und heißen Getränken nicht gestattet. Rauchen ist in der Jugendherberge nicht gestattet.
Der Konsum von mitgebrachten alkoholischen Getränken ist in der Jugendherberge und auf ihrem Gelände nicht erlaubt. Alkoholisierte Gäste können des Hauses verwiesen werden.
Tiere dürfen grundsätzlich nicht mitgebracht werden. Insbesondere Blinden- und Servicehunde können in Absprache mit der Herbergsleitung in der Jugendherberge bleiben. Die Landesverbände können für Hunde in ausgewiesenen Jugendherbergen weitere Ausnahmen zulassen.
Jugendherbergen sind in der Regel bis 22 Uhr geöffnet. Die Nachtruhe beginnt um 22 Uhr und endet um 7 Uhr. Um die Nachtruhe für andere Gäste zu ermöglichen, werden alle Gäste um Rücksicht gebeten. Bitte nehmen Sie bei Ihrem Aufenthalt Rücksicht auf andere Gäste, besonders wenn Sie elektronische Geräte benutzen.

Abreise

Die Schlafräume müssen bis 10 Uhr geräumt sein. Nach Absprache mit der Herbergsleitung sind Ausnahmen möglich.

www.jugendherberge.de

Check: Mediation

a) Vergleiche deine Antworten mit den Lösungen auf Seite 88 im Workbook.
b) Schätze deine Antworten mit einem grünen oder roten Gesicht ein.

1 Konntest du in Aufgabe 3 entsprechende *keywords* und *phrases* erkennen, die für die Lösung der Übung wichtig sind? ○ ○ → 1

2 Konntest du in Aufgabe 3 unbekannte Wörter mit Relativsätzen erklären? ○ ○ → 2

3 Konntest du in den Aufgaben 3 und 4 die Informationen auf Englisch geben? ○ ○ → 3

c) Wenn du dich rot eingeschätzt hast, schau dir die rechte Spalte an.
Die Nummern führen dich zu den passgenauen Übungen im Skills Training (S. 52–53).
Dort kannst du gezielt Mediation trainieren.

1 What you are allowed to do (Selecting relevant information from a written text) ➔ SF 1–2 (p. 64)

Scan the texts about Germany and answer the questions of your 15-year-old exchange student from Denmark. Mark the relevant keywords and sentences and answer the questions in English.

Geschäftsfähigkeit

Ausnahmsweise gibt es hier mal keinen Unterschied zwischen 14- und 16-Jährigen, ja noch nicht einmal zwischen 11- und 17-Jährigen! Von deinem siebten Lebensjahr an bis zu deinem achtzehnten Geburtstag bist du bedingt geschäftsfähig. Das heißt, du darfst dir Sachen kaufen, die du dir mit deinem üblichen Taschengeld leisten kannst. Wenn du von deinem Taschengeld eine größere Summe ansparst, sind auch etwas größere Ausgaben gesetzlich erlaubt. Ungültig werden Verträge jedoch, die eine größere Summe beinhalten, oder auch Langzeitverträge (z. B. bei Handys). In solchen Fällen benötigst du das Einverständnis eines Erziehungsberechtigten.

Jobben

Ab wann du dir etwas Taschengeld dazu verdienen darfst, steht nicht im Jugendschutzgesetz sondern im Jugendarbeitsschutzgesetz und das sagt, dass grundsätzlich niemand arbeiten darf, der jünger als 13 Jahre ist. Ab 13 Jahren sind dann leichte Arbeiten erlaubt. Das sind z. B. Zeitungen austragen oder Nachhilfestunden geben. Diese entgeltlichen Tätigkeiten dürfen aber nur zwischen 8 und 18 Uhr und nur mit Zustimmung eines Erziehungsberechtigten ausgeführt werden. Für Jugendliche ab 15 Jahren gilt dies nicht mehr. Sie dürfen nun bis zu vier Wochen Vollzeit (ca. 35–40 Stunden in der Woche) in den Ferien arbeiten. Erst ab 18 Jahren sind Akkord- und Nachtarbeit erlaubt.

Ins Kino gehen

[...] Für Filme kann es die Altersbeschränkungen ab 6, ab 12, ab 16 und ab 18 Jahren geben. Im Gegensatz zu einem Kneipenbesuch, werden diese Bestimmungen auch nicht aufgehoben oder gelockert, wenn ein Erziehungsberechtigter dabei ist. [...]. Darüber hinaus musst du wissen, dass du in Begleitung eines Erziehungsberechtigen sein musst, wenn du unter 14 Jahre bist und der Film nach 20 Uhr endet, du unter 16 Jahre bist und der Film nach 22 Uhr endet, du über 16 Jahre bist und der Film nach 24 Uhr endet.

www.deine-rechte.de

1 Could I get a job here in the holidays? How long could I work?

2 There's a horror film on at the *Max*, for over 16s. Can we see it?

3 Can a teenager sign a mobile contract[1] here or do you need your parents' permission?

TIP: Mark keywords in the questions. Then **scan** the paragraph headings to find out which has the relevant information. Then look for keywords in the paragraph.

2 Explaining words (Paraphrasing with a relative clause) ➔ SF 14 (p. 70)

If you don't know an important word in English, paraphrasing is very useful in mediation. Paraphrase words from exercise 3 of the Checkpoint with *It's a person/someone who ... It's something that ... It's a place where ... etc.*

TIP: Paraphrase with words you know. Often you know part of the word (z. B. Fahrrad, Sicherheit), or a word with a similar meaning.

1 Fahrradverleih: ______________________

2 Teilnehmer: ______________________

3 Sicherheitsunterweisung: ______________________

4 Helm: ______________________

5 Ureinwohner: ______________________

6 Wasserflugzeug: ______________________

[1] contract ['kɒntrækt] *Vertrag*

3 Saying it in a different way (Changing the sentence structure) ➜ *SF 12–15 (pp. 69–70)*

a) Here are some words/phrases/sentences from exercise 3 on page 51. If you don't know the words in English, express the meaning in a different way. There is more than one answer.

> **TIP:** When you mediate what someone says, you have to think quickly and use your own words, so keep it simple. Only the meaning is important, so you can change the sentence structure and the vocabulary of the original.

1 Die Teilnehmerzahl der Gruppe ist auf 12 Personen begrenzt.

____

2 fachkundig: ______________________________

3 unser erstes Ziel: ______________________________

4 Das Viertel ist richtig angesagt. ______________________________

5 Da haben wir eine Mittagspause eingelegt. ______________________________

____

6 Obwohl es teuer war, hat es sich gelohnt. ______________________________

____

Stanley Park

Lions Gate Bridge

The steam clock, Gastown

b) You can find the following sentences in the text of exercise 4 of the Checkpoint. Express the meaning in English with words you know. There is more than one answer.

1 Die Unterbringung erfolgt in Mehrbettzimmern. ______________________________

____

2 In Schlafräumen dürfen Speisen weder zubereitet noch gegessen werden. ______________________________

____

3 Die Nachtruhe beginnt um 22 Uhr und endet um 7 Uhr. ______________________________

____

4 Bitte nehmen Sie bei Ihrem Aufenthalt Rücksicht auf andere Gäste, besonders wenn Sie elektronische Geräte benutzen. ______________________________

____

1 Writing better texts (Using adjectives)

a) Choose adjectives from the box that you could use to describe 1–3 below.
Some adjectives fit into more than one list. You can add more useful adjectives to each list.

beautiful · boring · careful · colourful · competitive · creative · dangerous · decent · dreamy · easy-going · exciting · generous · hard-working · humid · intelligent · interested · lazy · lonely · loyal · mean · nervous · poisonous · polite · remote · responsible · rural · self-confident · sensitive · serious · spontaneous · talkative · tidy · tolerant · tropical · vast

1 about Australia: ______________________________

____

2 a partner in a relationship: ______________________________

____

3 an ideal job candidate: ______________________________

____

b) In your exercise book, write a short paragraph each about 1–3 in a) in which you give your personal opinion. Use eight to ten adjectives from the lists.

1 *I think Australia is a beautiful and exciting country. However, ...*

2 Climate change (Verb tenses) ➜ *GF 1 (pp. 75–78)*

Complete the text with verbs in the correct forms and tenses, active or passive.

For more than a century, people *have been using* (use) oil, coal and natural gas in vast amounts as energy. Over the years, carbon dioxide, a greenhouse gas which ____________ (trap) heat, ____________ (release) into the atmosphere. Without greenhouse gases, Earth ____________ (be) very cold, but people all over the world ____________ (produce) more greenhouse gases than the atmosphere ____________ (need) to stay at its normal temperature. As a result, Earth's average temperature ____________ (rise) and experts ____________ (believe) that this is the main reason why our climate ____________ (change). Sea levels ____________ (rise) because the ice at the poles ____________ (melt). If this continues, people in low-lying areas on coasts ____________ (lose) their homes because salt water ____________ (flood) cities such as London, New York or Hong Kong. Drinking water is already scarce in many parts of the world. In 2007, the south-east of the USA ____________ (hit) by a long period of extreme drought. In 2014, California ____________ (suffer) severely from water shortage because in the Sierra mountains it ____________ (snow) less than usual. These are just two examples of many.

3 Say it differently (Changing sentence structure)

When you summarize a text or mediate, you use your own words and express the meaning in a different way. Express the meaning of 1–5 differently. You can use the words in brackets ( ) or you can make your own changes.

1 Kim was watching her favourite TV show. Her phone rang in the middle of it. → (during)

Kim's phone rang during her favourite TV show.

2 It was her boyfriend. The last time he had phoned her was three days ago. → (for)

3 "I'm going to the new disco. Why don't you go with me?" he said. → (wanted)

4 The disco was full. However, the man at the door was friendly, so he let them in. → (although)

5 They didn't have much money. They shared a coke and a packet of crisps. → (Not …)

4 The Royal Flying Doctor Service (Joining sentences)

Choose a word from the brackets ( ) to join two sentences.
Change the order of the sentences only where necessary.

1 About 10 percent of the Australian population live in the outback.
They cannot get medical help easily. → (so that/so)

About 10 percent of the Australian population live in the outback, so they cannot get medical help easily.

2 Before the Royal Flying Doctor Service (RFDS) started, people in remote areas died. Doctors could not reach them.
→ (because/so)

3 The RFDS started over 90 years ago. It's a 24-hour service for rural and remote Australia.
→ (which/who)

4 The RFDS has established more than 30 bases. The service can reach people in over 90 percent of the country.
→ (so that/although)

5 It isn't easy to pass the tests and interviews. Lots of young people apply to the RFDS.
→ (although/when)

5 Australia today

a) 21 **Listening for gist:** listen once and tick (✓) the correct box.

The discussion is mainly about …

- ☐ global warming and greenhouse gases.
- ☐ marine algae.
- ☐ why corals are dying.

b) 21 **Listening for detail:** read the questions, then listen to the discussion again and make notes. Circle A, B or C.

1 Coral bleaching means that …

A corals grow old and change their colour.

B some corals turn white from the sunlight.

C corals lose their colours, become white and die.

2 The corals' colour and the energy that corals need to grow comes from …

A the corals themselves.

B marine algae.

C warm water temperatures.

3 Coral bleaching takes place because …

A the algae are destroyed.

B the coral is old.

C the coral stops growing.

4 The greatest danger to corals is …

A an increased water temperature.

B a big tropical storm.

C a rise in the sea level.

5 When the temperature rises, the bleaching process can start …

A after two months.

B after four weeks.

C immediately.

6 The Great Barrier Reef is …

A 900 miles long.

B 2,300 miles long.

C more than 1,400 miles long.

7 On the Great Barrier Reef there are about … different types of coral.

A nine hundred

B six hundred

C a thousand

6 The Red Centre

a) **Reading for gist:** skim the text and decide what it is about. Circle A, B or C.

A The history of Uluru **B** Aboriginal traditions **C** An Australian icon

Everybody knows it, everybody has seen postcards, pictures or videos about it, but to experience the feel and the spirit of Uluru, you have to go there yourself. It's a UNESCO World Heritage site, visited by at least half a million tourists every year. Visitors are amazed at the size and beauty of the site.

It stands in the southern part of Australia's Northern Territory, in the Uluru-Kata Tjuta National Park. It's a gigantic sandstone rock more than 360 m high, 3.5 km long and 2 km wide, surrounded by a vast area of desert. Geologists believe it to be about 550 million years old.

The rock is a photographer's paradise, especially at sunrise and sunset when the colours change to different shades of brown, red, orange and blue. Visitors willingly get up at or before 5 am. The car parks are full of people with photographic equipment. All are hoping to capture the various moods of the rock at sunrise.

So what else can you do there? A shopping trip? Well, not really. The nearest town is Alice Springs, 470 km away by road. It's a long, dry journey through the lonely outback to Uluru, but many tourists who fly to Alice Springs are prepared to do the 5-hour drive. There's also a small airport at Yulara, just twenty minutes from Uluru, which is used by thousands of visitors every year. It's also called the Ayers Rock Resort because it has hotels and camping sites, an information centre, a supermarket and other tourist facilities.

Uluru is also called Ayers Rock from colonial times. It was discovered in 1873 and was then named after the Australian Premier Henry Ayers. Uluru/Ayers Rock is now the official name for the sacred site of the Anangu, the Aboriginal people of the area who have lived there for over ten thousand years.

Because of their spiritual beliefs, the Anangu don't like visitors to climb Uluru. The guide books tell you it's permitted, so unfortunately about 20 percent of visitors do it, in spite of the Anangu warning sign 'Please don't climb'. The Anangu people want tourists to respect the Aboriginal culture and traditional law of their own free will, out of respect for the sacred site. There are also some special sacred parts of Uluru where tourists shouldn't take photos.

A further reason why the Anangu do not want visitors to climb Uluru is their concern for visitors' health. Some tourists do not pay attention to the warning. They do the climb against the will of the Anangu people even though they are not fit enough. The path that you climb is about 1.5 km long – that's about as high as a building with 95 stories. It's steep and dangerous too, especially when there are strong winds. In the summer months (December to March), temperatures can reach 40° C. More than 35 people have died of a heart attack because they climbed in the hot sun despite their health problems. Additionally, people who do the climb are often disappointed because from the top you see only desert. The beautiful views are from the base.

Instead of climbing the rock, visitors can walk around the base. The walk is about 10 km long, but it's flat, not difficult and much of it is under trees. Visitors can also hire a bicycle for a few hours or take their own bikes. There are various guided tours, often in air-conditioned coaches, and there's also a free short walk with an Aboriginal guide. It's about two kilometers there and back and takes about 90 minutes. During the walk, the guide tells you about Anangu culture, myths and legends, and Aboriginal rock paintings.

Remember, on any walk you need lots of water, sunscreen, a sunhat and good walking shoes!

b) Reading for detail: scan the text. Are the statements below true, false or is the information not in the text?

	True	False	Not in text
1 Uluru is located in a national park in South Australia.	◯	◯	◯
2 Visitors are fascinated by the rock's everchanging colours.	◯	◯	◯
3 The town Alice Springs is just an hour away by car.	◯	◯	◯
4 The Ayers Rock Resort is 18 km north of Uluru.	◯	◯	◯
5 The Ayers Rock Resort is at Yulara.	◯	◯	◯
6 Uluru was first called Ayers Rock in the nineteenth century.	◯	◯	◯
7 Henry Ayers was the man who discovered it.	◯	◯	◯
8 Uluru is owned by the Anangu people, but is leased and managed by Parks Australia.	◯	◯	◯
9 The walk around the base takes about four hours.	◯	◯	◯
10 Visitors can walk, cycle or go by bus around the rock.	◯	◯	◯
11 On average, one in five visitors climbs Uluru.	◯	◯	◯
12 The climb is safe in any kind of weather.	◯	◯	◯

c) Understanding the text: answer the questions.

1 Describe the problems of climbing Uluru in your own words.

____

____

____

____

____

____

____

2 Would you choose to do the climb? Why or why not? Give your reasons.

____

____

____

____

____

____

____

____

7 Talking about relationships

a) Look at the picture. Then complete tasks 1–2 below.
You should talk for about two to four minutes altogether.

1 Describe the picture. Make notes. Then record what you say.

2 Analyse and comment on the picture. What is the message of the picture?
Make notes. Then record what you say.

b) Look at the cartoon and complete the tasks.
You should talk for about two to four minutes.

1 Describe the cartoon. Make notes, then record what you say.

2 Analyse and comment on the cartoon. What is its message? Make notes, then record what you say.

c) Discuss the influence of social media/the computer on a relationship and/or in the family. Partner A thinks the influence is good, Partner B thinks it's bad. Try to sound polite although you disagree. You can use some of the following expressions:

- give reasons for your opinion:

  Let me explain why. In my opinion, ... This is how I feel.

- support your arguments with examples:

  I'll give you an example of what I mean. Another thing, ...

- say that you disagree:

  But I feel very strongly that ... That's not how I see it. I'm not sure if I share your view. There are more disadvantages than advantages.

- you can interrupt your partner:

  Sorry, but could I just say something?

- answer when your partner interrupts you:

  Yes, of course. Go ahead, please.

- point out your views that are the same:

  So we both agree that ...

- state your conclusions:

  To sum up, we could say that ... On a few points, I think we'll have to agree to differ.

8 Applying for a summer job

a) You would like to improve your English in the summer holidays. You find two interesting job offers on the internet and decide to apply for one of them. Choose A or B and write a letter of application on the computer. Use a correct layout and a suitable style.

A

– Summer Sales Support, London –

If you are interested in sales and customer service, this is an excellent opportunity to gain experience in a top retail environment in London.
We need reliable, confident and outgoing sales support for most departments, including sports and cosmetics. If you are hard-working, flexible and speak other languages, join our team.

Please note:
- You must have a fluent level of English.
- You must be available for at least 4 weeks from June to September.
- You should be willing to work shifts between 10 am and 6 pm and weekends.
- Previous sales experience would be an advantage but is not necessary.

We offer an exclusive workplace, a friendly team and discounts of 30 % on all goods.

Please send applications in writing to:
Sarah Jessop, Jarrods Recruitment,
182 Crompton Road, London SW1X OAZ, UK

B

– Wimbledon Animal Shelter –

If you would like to help with animal care and spend your summer vacation in London, voluntary work is a great way to do it. Our animal shelter was founded as a dogs' home in 1985 and has since grown to include many other animals. Charity organisations rely on volunteers.

For July and August, we need:
- an office assistant with good computer skills, e. g. for our website, newsletters, events and activities
- an assistant at reception, e. g. receiving and documenting new animals, showing visitors around the shelter, etc.
- practical hands-on helpers, e. g. for dog-walking, cleaning and feeding, general animal care, help with finding new homes for our animals

Whether you are considering a career in animal care or simply enjoy being with animals, contact us if you would like to be part of our team.
Accommodation and meals are provided. Applications from other countries are welcome.

Please write to:
Ian Wilks, Animal Shelter, 48 Victoria Rd.,
Wimbledon SW19 76L, UK

b) You tell a cousin in London about the two jobs and he/she decides to apply for the job in a) which you did not choose. For your cousin it will be the first job application.
Write an email to him/her with interview advice on the following points:

1 how to present himself/herself: personal qualities (strengths and weaknesses)

2 what information to give, e. g. school interests, free-time activities, details about job experience

3 possible career goals

4 why he/she would really like the job and is a good candidate for it

5 what to ask about the job

Dear …,

I think it's a good idea to apply for the job of … Be prepared for an interview – even by phone.
Think about what they might ask. Let me give you a few tips.

First, …
Remember to …
Don't …

9 Smartphone – friend or enemy

a) Your exchange student Chris in the UK has to write an essay with the title *Smartphones – for and against*. He asked you for help. You find the following article in the magazine *Teen Express*. Read the article and mark relevant sentences.

Es sieht so aus, als könnte man ohne Smartphone in unserer modernen Gesellschaft kaum auskommen. Ob in der Bahn, im Bus, im Café oder auf der Straße ist die massenhafte Nutzung von Handys und Tablets überall präsent. Man kann nicht leugnen, dass die Erfindung eine Menge Vorteile mit sich bringt, die unseren Alltag erleichtern. Man hat alles in einem kleinen, handlichen Gerät: Telefon, Internet, Kamera, Video-Kamera, Navi, Musik, Filme, Spiele und unzählige Apps, die alles können – immer dabei und immer einsatzbereit.
Aber es gibt auch Nachteile. Der Mensch ist von Natur aus neugierig und oft ungeduldig. Egal, wo man ist oder was man gerade macht, sobald das Handy vibriert oder blinkt, wird meist voller Erwartung aufs Display gestarrt. Will man sich mal eine Ruhepause gönnen, klingelt es woanders – und so wird man oft unfreiwilliger Mithörer eines peinlichen Gesprächs zwischen Menschen, die man nicht kennt. Was kann man dagegen tun? Wird es nicht irgendwann zu viel?

Die Wörter *Sucht* und *Abhängigkeit* bringt man meist mit Rauchen, Alkohol, Drogen oder Glücksspiel in Verbindung. Aber ist das bedenkliche Verhalten vieler Mitmenschen ihrem Handy gegenüber keine Sucht? Wer verzichtet freiwillig ein paar Stunden auf sein Handy? Wer schaltet sein Handy überhaupt aus ohne das Gefühl zu haben, dass etwas fehlt? Das Gefühl zu haben, dass man nicht ständig erreichbar ist, stellt für einige Menschen oft ein ernsthaftes Problem dar. Und wenn mal das Handy irgendwo liegen bleibt oder verloren geht, dann ist eine kleine Katastrophe schon vorprogrammiert, oder?

Noch wird exzessiver Medienkonsum zu wenig ernst genommen, weil die Auswirkungen von den Betroffenen heruntergespielt werden. Meist sind es junge Menschen, die, ohne es zu merken, die Kontrolle über das Ausmaß ihrer Mobilfunk-Nutzung verlieren. Computer, Smartphone und Tablet nehmen im Leben eines Teenagers oft einen wichtigeren Platz ein als Hausaufgaben oder Sport.

In letzter Zeit hat es einige Studien gegeben, die versucht haben, das wahre Ausmaß dieser elektronischen Mediensucht zu untersuchen. Was sind die typischen Anzeichen einer Handy-Sucht? Hier einige interessante Feststellungen:

1. Man lässt sich von dem Handy gern ablenken – auch bei Hausaufgaben oder wichtigen Lernaufgaben. Man kann nicht nein sagen.
2. Nach dem Aufwachen wird als erstes das Handy eingeschaltet.
3. Sogar im Badezimmer ist das Handy dabei.
4. Man ist psychisch nicht in der Lage, die zwanghaften Handy-Aktivitäten zu begrenzen.
5. Unproduktive WhatsApp- und Messenger-Dienste haben Vorrang. Man muss einfach online sein, um nichts zu verpassen.
6. Man ist gelangweilt, wenn das Handy mal nicht klingelt.
7. Zeit mit Familie und Freunden wird oft auf ein Minimum reduziert.
8. Beim Treffen mit Freunden ist das Handy immer präsent und wird auch ständig bedient. Man redet oft mehr mit dem Handy als mit echten Gesprächspartnern.
9. Man spielt oft stundenlang, auch die ganze Nacht durch, um das nächste Level eines Spiels zu erreichen. Man hat keine Ruhe, bis es geschafft ist.

Vielleicht denkt ihr mal über euer eigenes Verhalten im Umgang mit Handy und Co nach. Die meisten der oben beschriebenen neun Punkte treffen sicherlich nicht auf euch zu, oder …?

Source: Teen Express, 2017

b) Write an email to Chris in which you summarize ideas for and against smartphones, which you have read about in the article in a).

Hi Chris,

I've just read about the topic in a magazine, so maybe I can help you with a few ideas.
First, the advantages: …

10 Chat at the sports centre

Your US cousin Ryan is visiting you. You take him to your local sports centre where you meet Jakub, a friend who speaks German better than English. Mediate for Ryan and Jakub. Make notes in English and German.

You: Hi, Jakub. Mein Cousin Ryan aus Atlanta ist bei uns zu Besuch.
Er mag Sport über alles, also habe ich ihn heute zum Training mitgebracht.

Jakub: Hello, Ryan. Willkommen. Seit wann bist du hier und wie lange bleibst du in Deutschland?

You: *He wants to know how long you've been here and* ______________________

Ryan: Tell him I'm here for the summer vacation. It's really cool in Germany. Nice people.

You: *Er sagt,* ______________________

Jakub: Atlanta ist in Georgia, oder? Da wurde doch Martin Luther King geboren – haben wir in der Schule gelernt. Sag ihm, ich war noch nie in den USA, aber mein Onkel wohnt in New York. Meine Schwester und ich möchten ihn gern besuchen, aber zuerst müssen wir Geld sparen. Was für Sport treibt man in New York? Weiß Ryan das?

You: *He says* ______________________

____

____

Ryan: Tell him in New York the main sport is baseball. Maybe he knows the Yankees and the Mets, both major league. My favourite baseball team is the Atlanta Braves. My dream is to get a sport scholarship for either baseball or football and be a student athlete. But it's very difficult. Being talented isn't enough. You have to be really hard-working, self-confident, competitive, really crazy about your sport and very serious about achieving your goal. You need luck too.

You: *Er sagt* ______________________

____

____

Jakub: Wow, finde ich toll. Ich mag Fußball, aber so ehrgeizig bin ich nicht. Ich brauche Zeit für andere Sachen. Sag Ryan, ich spiele Lead-Gitarre in einer Band – macht viel Spaß. Wir schreiben eigene Songs und nächsten Samstag spielen wir im Jugendzentrum. Ich lade euch gern dazu ein!

You: ______________________

____

____

Jakub: Da kommen unser Trainer und die anderen Jungs. Ryan darf sicher heute mitspielen – hoffentlich auf unserer Seite, dann gewinnen wir bestimmt.

You: ______________________

____

____

SF 1 Skimming and scanning ➔ *SB (p. 123)*

Skimming

Skimming hilft, schnell zu sehen, ob ein Text für deinen Zweck geeignet ist.

Step 1: Sieh dir diese Textteile an, um zu sehen, worum es im Text geht:
- Überschrift und Unterüberschriften
- Bilder und Bildunterschriften
- den ersten Satz jedes Absatzes – dieser Satz ist meist der *topic sentence*, der die Hauptidee des Absatzes nennt
- den letzten Absatz des Textes, der oft eine Zusammenfassung des Textes enthält

Step 2: Fasse für dich selbst den Text in ein paar Worten zusammen. Wenn dir das ohne Probleme gelingt, dann weißt du, um was es in dem Text geht – und dass dein Skimming erfolgreich war.

TIPP: Mach dir um unbekannten Wortschatz erstmal keine Gedanken – dafür ist Zeit, wenn du feststellst, dass der Text für dich geeignet ist.

Scanning

Scanning hilft, in einem Text schnell nach bestimmten Informationen zu suchen.

Step 1: Überlege dir *keywords*. Suchst du z. B. nach den Öffnungszeiten eines Museums, könnten das Wörter sein wie *open*, *hours* oder *days*.

Step 2: Überfliege den Text und suche nach den *keywords*. Du kannst dabei mit dem Finger in einer „S-Form" durch den Text gehen.

Step 3: Lies die Textstelle, die dein *keyword* enthält, um zu sehen, ob sie die gewünschten Informationen enthält. Wenn nicht, scanne weiter.

TIPP: Wenn du mit Texten im Internet arbeitest, kann dein Browser dir viel Arbeit abnehmen.
Mit **Strg+F** (**Cmd+F** am Mac) kannst du nach deinen *keywords* suchen und nur die Textstellen lesen, in denen ein *keyword* markiert ist.

SF 2 Marking up a text ➔ *SB (p. 123)*

Step 1: Lies die Aufgabe genau und überlege, welche Informationen du zur Beantwortung brauchst. Behalte dies beim Lesen des Textes im Kopf.

Step 2: Markiere nur Informationen, die wichtig sind (z. B. durch Unterstreichen, Einkreisen oder Markieren mit einem Textmarker). Oft reicht es, nur ein oder zwei Wörter in einem Satz zu markieren.

Step 3: Mach dir kurze Notizen am Rand – z. B. kurze Überschriften oder Stichwörter –, die den Inhalt kurz zusammenfassen.

TIPP:
1. Verwende unterschiedliche Farben für unterschiedliche Aufgaben/ Fragestellungen.
2. Markiere wirklich nur Stichwörter, sonst wird es unübersichtlich.

SF 3 The stages of writing ➔ *SB (p. 124)*

Planungsphase

Step 1: Plane ausreichend Zeit ein und denke über folgende Fragen nach:
- Über welches Thema willst du schreiben?
- Was sollst du tun (beschreiben, erläutern, zusammenfassen …)?
- Welche Dinge musst du für den geforderten Text beachten?

Step 2: Dann solltest du
- alle nötigen Informationen für dein Thema **recherchieren**, (➔ *SF 28*)
- Ideen/Argumente sammeln und sortieren
- und eine Gliederung (**Outline**) für den Text (z. B. einen Bericht) machen. (➔ *SF 6*)

Entwurfsphase

Jetzt schreibe deinen ersten Entwurf:
- Füge deiner Outline **linking words** (➔ *SF 5*) und **topic sentences** hinzu (➔ *SF 4*).
- Beginne für jede neue Idee einen neuen Absatz.
- Führe deine Ideen aus und gib Beispiele (wenn das die Textsorte erfordert).
- Denk über das Ende deines Textes nach. Wenn du weißt, wie dein Text endet, ist es leichter, eine gute Einleitung zu schreiben, die darauf hinführt. (➔ *SF 4*)

TIPP: Mehr Informationen zum Verfassen guter Texte findest du auch in den folgenden Abschnitten:
- SF 4: Structuring texts
- SF 5: Writing good sentences
- SF 6: Making an outline
- SF 7: Writing a report
- SF 8: Writing a summary
- SF 9: Argumentative writing
- SF 10: Writing a formal letter or email
- SF 11: Revising texts
- SF 28: Internet research

Überarbeitungsphase

- Liest sich der Text gut? Ist er logisch aufgebaut? Hat er eine **gute Struktur**? (➜ *SF 4*)
- Prüfe die **sprachlichen Aspekte** deines Textes: Grammatik, Rechtschreibung, Zeichensetzung, Ausdruck, *linking words*, *time markers*, etc. (➜ *SF 5, SF 11*)
- Schreibe deinen Text noch einmal ab. Verbessere alles, was im ersten Entwurf noch nicht ganz gepasst hat. Wenn du **Feedback** von jemand anderem bekommen hast, sieh es dir genau an und entscheide dann, was davon du für deinen Text übernehmen möchtest.

SF 4 Structuring texts ➜ *SB (p. 125)*

Struktur

Ein guter Text besteht in der Regel aus drei Teilen:

- Einleitung (*introduction*):
  Hier steht, worum es in dem Text geht. An dieser Stelle kann auch ein Problem genannt werden, das in dem Text erörtert werden soll.
- Hauptteil (*main body*):
  Dieser Teil ist in mehrere Absätze gegliedert und präsentiert die Details (Fakten, Beispiele etc.) zu deinem Thema.
- Schluss (*conclusion*):
  Hier gibst du deinem Text ein passendes Ende.

Absätze

Längere Texte sind einfacher zu lesen und schneller zu verstehen, wenn sie in Absätze eingeteilt sind. Dabei solltest du folgende Dinge beachten:

- Fange für neue Aspekte einen neuen Absatz an.
- Beginne mit einem interessanten *topic sentence*.
- Beende deinen Text im letzten Absatz mit einer Zusammenfassung oder etwas Persönlichem.

Einleitungssätze

Jeder Absatz sollte mit einem Einleitungssatz beginnen.
Dieser *topic sentence* beschreibt, worum es in dem Absatz geht. Wichtige Dinge, die du in einem *topic sentence* ansprechen kannst, sind z. B.

- **Orte:** *My trip to Berlin was exciting.*
- **Personen:** *The Beatles are a famous band.*
- **Aktivitäten:** *Lots of people ride their bike every day.*

My Trip to Wales

Last summer I wanted to go to Wales because I like the mountains.

First I had to find some information on Wales. So I went to the library and looked for books about Wales. I found a book with some interesting information on hiking tours and I also found a camping guide for Wales. I went home with three books under my arm.

At home I started to plan for my trip. I read all the books and took notes on hiking trails, the weather and the equipment I would need for camping and hiking. After a few days I knew where I wanted to go and what I wanted to do there.

I did not want to go to Wales alone, so I had to find someone to go with me. I called most of my friends and told them about my plan. Some of them did not want to go hiking and others had no money for the trip. But my friend Judith agreed to go with me. We decided to go in late August.

Judith and I spent two lovely weeks in Wales. We went to Snowdonia and enjoyed the fantastic mountains. We stayed in a lovely bed and breakfast and met lots of really nice people. Before we went home we spent two very interesting days in Cardiff.

This was one of the best summer holidays I ever had. Go to Wales – it's fantastic!

SF 5 Writing good sentences ➜ *SB (pp. 125–126)*

Die folgenden Techniken helfen dir, dich variabel auszudrücken und damit den Stil deiner Texte zu verbessern.

Adjektive

Verwende Adjektive, wenn du Dinge, Orte und Menschen näher beschreiben möchtest:

- *a **bright** face*
- *a **fantastic** trip*

Stell aber sicher, dass du die Adjektive **good**, **bad** und **nice** nicht zu häufig einsetzt. Ersetze sie durch andere Adjektive mit einer ähnlichen bzw. genaueren Bedeutung:

- *a **nice** teacher: a **friendly** teacher, a **helpful** teacher, …*
- *a **good** book: an **interesting** book, a **funny** book, …*

Adverbien

Verwende Adverbien, um Handlungen näher zu beschreiben:

- *They walked home* ***slowly****.*
- *She talked* ***quietly****.*

Verwende Ausdrücke wie **really**, **very**, **a bit** etc., um Aussagen zu verdeutlichen oder zu verstärken:

- *It was a* ***really*** *sad story.*
- *The houses are* ***very*** *high.*

Konjunktionen

Konjunktionen wie **and**, **but** oder **because** geben deinen Sätzen eine klare, gut nachvollziehbare Struktur:

- *We went to the London Eye, but it was* ***very*** *expensive.*

Relativsätze

Relativsätze verbinden Sätze oder geben mehr Informationen zu einer Sache oder einer Person:

- *This is the shop* ***which*** *sells the best ice cream in Berlin.*

Zeitangaben

Time markers/adverbiale Bestimmungen der Zeit helfen dem Leser, sich in einem Text oder einer Geschichte zeitlich zurechtzufinden. Verwende *time markers*, um …

- die **Reihenfolge von Ereignissen** zu verdeutlichen:
  at first, next, finally, …
- zu zeigen, **wie viel Zeit** zwischen einzelnen Ereignissen vergeht:
  for half an hour, just two minutes later, …
- zu verdeutlichen, **wie langsam oder schnell** etwas passiert:
  immediately, it took hours, faster than I could look, …
- zu sagen, wenn etwas **zeitgleich** passiert:
  while I was waiting, during the lesson, as we came round the corner, …
- die **Ereignisse eines Textes/einer Geschichte** zeitlich einzuordnen:
  two summers ago, last Halloween, on my way home from school yesterday, …

SF 6 Making an outline ➔ *SB (p. 126)*

Jede Art von Text profitiert davon, wenn du dir vorab überlegst, was du in welcher Reihenfolge schreiben willst.

- Wenn du einen Bericht schreiben sollst (➔ *SF 7*), kann es helfen, die wichtigsten Punkte schon in der **Gliederung** zu berücksichtigen: eine gute **Struktur** und die Beantwortung der ***wh*****-Fragen**.
- Bei einer Zusammenfassung (➔ *SF 8*) kannst du hier die wichtigsten Punkte festhalten.
- Für eine Erörterung (➔ *SF 9*) kannst du in deiner Outline schon die Argumente sortieren, die du im Text bringen möchtest.

Damit leistest du schon eine Menge Vorarbeit und erleichterst dir das Schreiben.

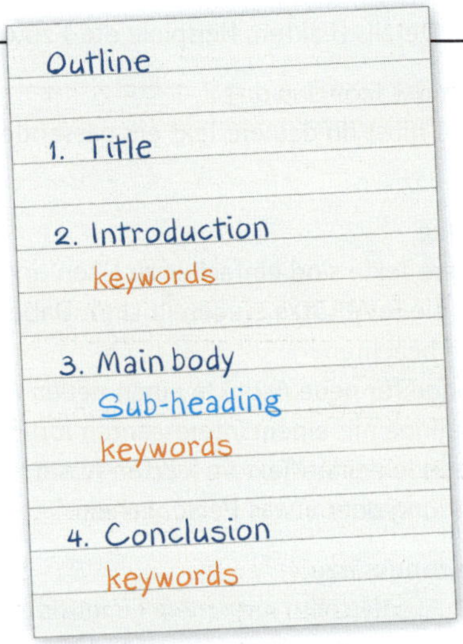

SF 7 Writing a report ➔ *SB (p. 127)*

Struktur

Wie jeder Text sollte ein Bericht aus einer **Überschrift**, einer **Einleitung**, einem **Hauptteil** und einem **Schluss** bestehen. (➔ *SF 4*)

In einer Gliederung (➔ *SF 6*) kannst du diese Struktur schon anlegen und für jeden Textteil eine Überschrift notieren sowie Stichwörter dazu ergänzen. Wenn du viele Informationen im Hauptteil unterbringen möchtest, verwende auch Unterüberschriften.

Stichwörter

In der **Einleitung** eines Berichtes sagst du kurz, was passiert ist. Dabei kannst du schon knapp die wichtigsten ***wh*****-Fragen** beantworten, bevor du im Hauptteil näher darauf eingehst.

In deiner Gliederung (➔ *SF 6*) solltest du deswegen für die Einleitung deine Stichworte auf die Fragen **Who?**, **What?**, **When?**, **Where?** und **Why?** konzentrieren.

Im **Hauptteil** eines Berichtes stehen dann die **Details** des Ereignisses, meist in chronologischer Reihenfolge. Hier werden also die *wh*-Fragen genauer beantwortet, deswegen solltest du in der Gliederung für den Hauptteil weitere Stichworte zu den einzelnen Fragen sammeln.

Im **Schlussabsatz** bringst du deinen Bericht zum Abschluss, indem du z. B. kurz das Ergebnis oder die Folgen des beschriebenen Ereignisses darstellst.

TIPP: Ein Bericht soll objektiv sein und Fakten darstellen. Konzentriere dich bei deinen *keywords* in der Gliederung darauf, die 5 *wh*-Fragen zu beantworten:

- **What** happened?
- **Who** did what?
- **When** did it happen?
- **Where** did it happen?
- **Why** did it happen?

Denk daran, dass ein Bericht im *simple past* geschrieben wird. Du solltest also deine Stichworte auch gleich so notieren.

SF 8 Writing a summary ➔ *SB (pp. 127–128)*

Planungsphase

Step 1: Lies den Text genau. Mach dir Notizen oder markiere wichtige Stellen im Text (➔ *SF 2*).

Step 2: Beantworte die *wh*-Fragen **Who? What? Where? When? Why?** zum Text. Du kannst dir dazu Stichworte am Rand machen.

Who? Who does something? Who is the text about?
What? What happens? What does person X do?
Where? Where does it take place?
When? When does it take place?
Why? Why does person X act this way? Why does something happen?

Step 3: Entscheide, welche Textteile wichtige Informationen enthalten. Beispiele, Vergleiche, direkte Rede oder Zahlen und Ähnliches gehören nicht in eine Zusammenfassung.

Schreibphase

Step 1: Schreib einen ersten Entwurf.
- Beginne mit der Einleitung, in der wichtige Informationen wie Titel, Autor/in, Thema und Hauptaussage des Textes stehen. Wenn du einen Artikel zusammenfasst, solltest du hier die Quelle nennen.
- Verwende immer das **simple present**.
- Kopiere nicht den Text, sondern benutze deine eigenen Worte.
- Wichtig: gib nie deine eigene Meinung oder Wertung.

Step 2: Überarbeite deine Zusammenfassung.
- Hast du alle wichtigen Aspekte genannt? Hast du unwichtige Details weggelassen?
- Ist der Text durchgängig *im simple present*? Sind die Textteile gut verbunden? Ist der Text logisch aufgebaut und gut zu verstehen?
- Vergiss nicht, Rechtschreibung/Grammatik zu prüfen. (➔ *SF 11*)

TIPP: Du kannst Teile, die für deine Zusammenfassung überflüssig sind, im Text einklammern.

LANGUAGE HELP: Folgende *phrases* können dir bei der **Einleitung** helfen:
- The story/text is about …
- The text deals with …
- The topic of the text is …
- The article/text shows …

SF 9 Argumentative writing ➔ *SB (pp. 128–129)*

Planungsphase

Step 1: Lies die Aufgabe sorgfältig durch.

Step 2: Sammle Ideen und mache erste Notizen. Schreibe alle Argumente pro und contra auf, die dir einfallen.

Step 3: Ordne deine Argumente, z. B. in Form einer Outline. (➔ *SF 6*) Hebe das Argument hervor, das deine Position am besten unterstreicht – damit solltest du deinen Hauptteil beenden, denn das merken sich die Leser am ehesten.

Schreibphase

Step 1: Schreibe deine Einleitung: sage kurz, um welches Thema es geht, ohne deine eigene Meinung dazu zu äußern.

Step 2: Im Hauptteil präsentierst du die Argumente, die du dir überlegt hast. Dabei helfen folgende Redemittel:
- **Presenting arguments:** *One of the main reasons why …* • *It is often said that …* • *Some people think …* • *In addition to these points …*
- **Ordering arguments:** *In the first place, …* • *Firstly,/Secondly,/Thirdly, …* • *Finally, …* • *First of all …*
- **Contrasting arguments:** *On the one hand – on the other hand* • *Contrary to what most people believe, …* • *While/Although …*
- **Giving examples:** *For example, …* • *This is clear because …*

Step 3: Am Schluss fasst du deine Argumente nochmal kurz zusammen und erklärst deine Schlussfolgerung:
- **Summing up arguments:** *To sum up, …* • *In conclusion, …* • *All in all, …* • *I would like to finish by pointing out again that …*
- **Explaining your conclusion:** *After looking at both sides of the argument …* • *Although I understand the other side of the argument, I still think …* • *Personally, I believe that …*

Outline/Notes

1. Introduction
introduce the topic

2. Main body
1st paragraph: arguments contra
- argument 1
- argument 2, etc.
2nd/3rd paragraph: arguments pro
- argument 1
- argument 2, etc.
end with strongest argument!

4. Conclusion
sum up your arguments
give your opinion

TIPP: Deine Argumente wirken überzeugender, wenn du:
- dich wo möglich auf deine eigenen Erfahrungen berufst,
- Fakten (Quellen, Experten, Statistiken usw.) präsentierst: *It can't be denied that …, It's a fact that …, It goes without saying that …*

SF 10 Writing a formal letter or email ➜ *SB (p. 129)*

Wenn du einen Brief an eine Organisation, einen potenziellen Arbeitgeber oder eine Universität schreibst, sollte dein Brief gewissen formalen Regeln folgen.

Schreibe **deine Adresse** (ohne Namen) oben rechts. Verwende keine typisch deutschen Buchstaben wie ä, ö, ü oder ß.

Schreibe die volle Anschrift (mit Namen, wenn du ihn weißt) des **Adressaten** auf die linke Seite.

Schreibe das **Datum** auf die rechte Seite.

Sage kurz im **Betreff**, worum es im Brief geht.

Beginne deinen Brief mit *Dear Sir or Madam*, wenn du keinen genauen Ansprechparntner hast. Ansonsten schreibe *Dear Mr/Mrs/Ms …* (ohne Komma danach!). Fange danach immer groß an.

Nenne den **Grund des Schreibens** im ersten Absatz.

- Ergänze weitere Informationen in den folgenden Absätzen.
- Verwende **Langformen** (*I am/We are/I would*) statt **Kurzformen** (*I'm/We're/I'd*) und Abkürzungen.

Wenn du den Adressaten um etwas bittest (z. B. Informationen), **bedanke dich** im Voraus.

Beende den Brief mit *Yours faithfully* wenn du den Namen des Ansprechpartners kennst; ansonsten schreibe *Yours sincerely*. Tippe deinen Namen am Ende des Briefes, aber lasse ausreichend Platz für deine **Unterschrift**.

Kruemelstrasse 12
12345 Berlin
Germany

John Keats
Donne House
Ipswich IP3 4BA
United Kingdom

3 March 2016

Enquiry about exchange programme

Dear Mr Keats

I am writing to enquire about the exchange programme which I saw advertised in The English Magazine.

I have been studying English at school for five years now and I would like to take part in an exchange programme to improve my English.

Could you please tell me if you offer any exchange programmes for one month in the summer? It would be helpful to know about dates, application procedures and the cost of such an exchange. Any additional information would be very welcome.

Thank you for your help. I look forward to hearing from you soon.

Yours sincerely,

Paul Panther

Paul Panther

TIPP: Bei einer formellen E-Mail brauchst du Datum und Adressaten nicht zu nennen. Ansonsten gelten dieselben Regeln wie bei einem formellen Brief. Liste am Ende der Mail deine Kontaktdaten auf (Name, Adresse, ggf. Telefonnummer). Ganz wichtig: verwende auf keinen Fall Emoticons oder Smileys.

SF 11 Revising texts ➜ *SB (p. 130)*

Textüberarbeitung

1. **Stimmt die Struktur?** (➜ *SF 4*)
   Jeder Text braucht
   - eine Einleitung, die in das Thema einführt,
   - einen Hauptteil, der das Thema ausführt,
   - einen Schluss, der alles auf den Punkt bringt.
2. **Stimmt der Aufbau der Absätze?** (➜ *SF 4*)
   Jeder Absatz
   - befasst sich mit einem zusammenhängenden Gedanken,
   - beginnt mit einem *topic sentence*, der diesen Gedanken einführt.
3. **Stimmen die Verknüpfungen?** (➜ *SF 5*)
   Gute *linking words*
   - schaffen Verbindungen zwischen Sätzen oder Satzteilen,
   - helfen, Zusammenhänge besser darzustellen und verständlich zu machen.
4. **Sind die Zeitangaben richtig gesetzt?** (➜ *SF 5*)
   Time markers
   - helfen, sich z. B. in einer Geschichte zurechtzufinden,
   - machen das Geschehen anschaulicher.
5. **Enthält der Text Adjektive und Adverbien?** (➜ *SF 5*)
   Adjektive und Adverbien
   - erlauben nähere Beschreibungen von Personen und Dingen,
   - machen Texte anschaulicher.
6. **Hat der Text sprachliche/grammatikalische Fehler?**
   Überprüfe deinen Text
   - auf Rechtschreibung,
   - auf grammatische Formen, z. B. Verbformen, Satzbau (*word order*) usw.

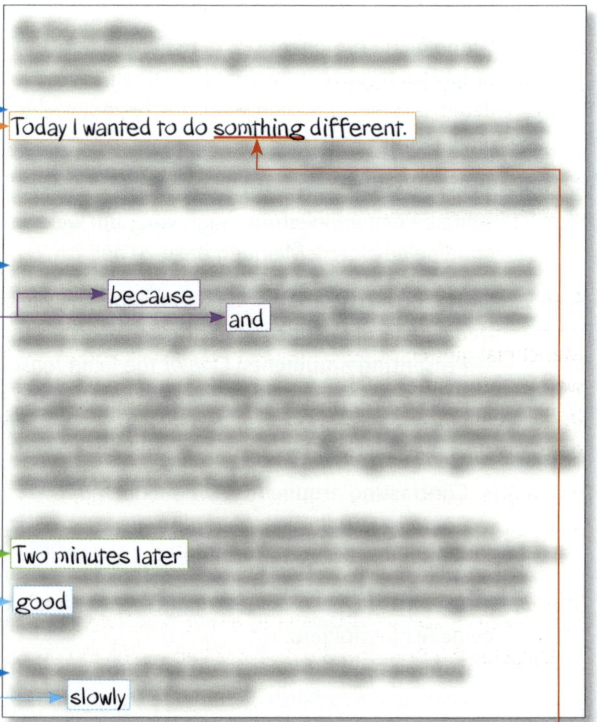

Fehlerprotokoll

Die Fehler in einem Text zu korrigieren ist eine Sache, aber besser wäre es natürlich, dieselben Fehler nicht zu wiederholen.

Dabei hilft ein Fehlerprotokoll. Darin notierst du Fehler, die du immer wieder machst. Dieses Fehlerprotokoll kann ein Heft sein, ein Karteikasten oder auch eine Sammlung von Notizzetteln, die du dir über deinen Schreibtisch hängst.

Hauptsache, es ist etwas, das du immer schnell zur Hand hast, wenn du zu Hause einen Text schreiben oder überarbeiten sollst.

TIPP: Häufige Fehlerquellen sind z. B.
- Groß-/Kleinschreibung
- Wörter, die gleich klingen, aber unterschiedlich geschrieben werden: *your/you're, their/they're/there*
- Verwendung des Apostrophs
- Bildung der Zeitformen der Verben: *stop* → *stopping, try* → *tries*
- Wörter mit „stummen" Buchstaben: *walk, talk, know*

SF 12 Mediating written or spoken information ➜ *SB (p. 131)*

Nicht jeder spricht und versteht sowohl Deutsch als auch Englisch; daher kann es vorkommen, dass du in bestimmten Situationen für Andere zwischen den Sprachen vermitteln musst – das nennt man dann **Mediation**.

Wie und was genau du vermitteln musst, hängt von der Situation ab und auch davon, ob du den Inhalt eines geschriebenen Textes wiedergeben oder zwischen zwei Sprechern vermitteln sollst.

Sprachmittlung bedeutet nicht Übersetzen (von Texten) oder Dolmetschen (bei Unterhaltungen), sondern das sinngemäße Übertragen von Inhalten in die andere Sprache.

Mediation von schriftlichen oder mündlichen Informationen

Wenn du Informationen in einer anderen Sprache wiedergeben sollst, geht es nicht darum, alles zu übersetzen, sondern es kommt darauf an, die wichtigsten Informationen herauszusuchen. Oft stellt dir die Person, für die du die Informationen wiedergibst, gezielte Fragen – so weißt du, worauf du achten musst.

Schriftliche Informationen
- **Scanne** den Text gezielt nach den geforderten Informationen. (➜ *SF 1*)
- Mach dir keine Sorgen, wenn du nicht jedes Wort verstehst. Das ist oft nicht nötig, um die wichtigen Punkte zu verstehen und wiederzugeben.
- Wenn der Text länger ist und du viele Informationen im Blick behalten musst, **markiere** die wichtigsten Textstellen. (➜ *SF 2*)
- Mach dir **Notizen** in deinen eigenen Worten.

Mündliche Informationen
- Achte beim Hören gezielt auf die gesuchten Informationen. (➜ *SF 22*)
- Mach dir Notizen.
- Überlege, wie du deine Notizen am besten in der anderen Sprache wiedergeben kannst.

TIPP: Bei **Mediation im Unterricht** hast du in der Regel eine Aufgabenstellung, die dir sagt, worauf du beim Lesen oder Hören achten musst bzw. welche Stellen du wiedergeben sollst. Konzentriere dich beim Lesen des Textes auf diese Stellen (*scanning*) bzw. mache dir gezielt zu diesen Stellen Notizen.

TIPP: Wenn du den Inhalt eines Texts schriftlich in einer anderen Sprache wiedergeben sollst, achte darauf, dass deine Mediation nicht länger ist als ca. 35–40 % des Originaltextes, ähnlich wie bei einer *summary*. (➜ *SF 8*)

SF 13 Selecting relevant information *SB (p. 131)*

Manchmal gibt es keine gezielten Fragen oder Aufgabenstellungen, die dir sagen, welche Informationen du aus einem Text heraussuchen und wiedergeben sollst.
In der Regel hast du aber trotzdem Anhaltspunkte, die sich aus der Situation ergeben oder aus dem, was dir dein Gegenüber erzählt hat.

Wenn du in einer solchen Situation bist, helfen folgende Hinweise:
- **Analysiere die Situation**, um abzuschätzen, um welche Informationen es gehen könnte (Restaurant, Bahnhof, Flughafen usw.).
- Wenn du unsicher bist, **frage nach**.
- **Übersetze** wichtige Stichworte direkt, wenn du die Wörter kennst.
- **Umschreibe Begriffe**, die du nicht kennst. (➜ *SF 14*)

TIPP: Wenn du Informationen wiedergibst, kannst du oft Details zu einem Begriff zusammenfassen. Wenn z. B. in einem Text twitter, facebook und Pinterest vorkommen, kannst du *social media* sagen anstatt alle aufzuzählen.

SF 14 Paraphrasing ➔ *SB (p. 132)*

Es fällt dir eventuell manchmal schwer, Informationen in Englisch wiederzugeben, z. B. weil

- dein Wortschatz nicht ausreicht,
- dir bekannte Wörter in der Situation nicht einfallen
- oder spezielle Fachbegriffe auftauchen.

Wenn dir das passiert, dann solltest du versuchen, diese Wörter zu umschreiben, z. B. mithilfe von Relativsätzen wie:
It's somebody/a person who …
It's something that you use to …
It's an animal that …
It's a place that/where …

LANGUAGE HELP: Oft helfen beim Umschreiben auch **Synonyme** (gleiche Bedeutung) oder **Antonyme** (gegenteilige Bedeutung). Wenn du die weißt, kannst du z. B. sagen:

- It's the same as …
- It's the opposite of …

SF 15 Cultural differences ➔ *SB (p. 132)*

Wenn du anderen Menschen hilfst, Texte oder Gehörtes zu verstehen, kann es neben Wortschatzproblemen auch noch andere Schwierigkeiten geben. Diese sind häufig in **kulturellen Unterschieden** begründet. Um hier helfen zu können, musst du dir beim Sprachmitteln bewusst machen, dass dein Gegenüber evtl. bestimmte Dinge nicht weiß, die für dich selbstverständlich sind, oder dass er/sie dich nicht sofort versteht, obwohl du den Inhalt korrekt übertragen hast.

Dinge, die häufig zu **Missverständnissen** führen, sind z. B.

- **Temperaturen:** 30 Grad bei uns sind heiß, in den USA eher kalt, weil in den USA Temperaturen in Fahrenheit angegeben werden, nicht in Celsius.
- **Längenangaben/Geschwindigkeit:** Bei uns wird das metrische System verwendet (Meter, Kilometer usw.), in den USA das *imperial system* mit *inch*, *yard* und *mile*. Das kann auch bei Geschwindigkeitsangaben zu Verwirrung führen, denn 75 *mph* (Meilen pro Stunde) sind z. B. ca. 120 km/h.

Am besten ist es, wenn du immer noch mal höflich nachfragst, ob dein Gegenüber alles verstanden hat. Wenn du dann feststellst, dass es zu einem Missverständnis gekommen ist, dann kannst du folgende Dinge probieren:

- Frage höflich nach, wo das Missverständnis ist.
- Versuche, das Missverständnis durch eine neue Erklärung zu beseitigen.
- Ergänze deine Erläuterung evtl. mit **Hintergrundinformationen**: Es kann sein, dass du bestimmte Dinge, die für dich völlig normal sind, erklären musst (wie z. B. Mülltrennung oder das Benutzen des Nahverkehrs).
- Sei auch offen für die Erklärungen, die du evtl. im Gegenzug bekommst – hier kannst du Dinge über das Land deines Gegenübers lernen.

TIPP: Es hilft, wenn du versuchst, mögliche "Stolperstellen" schon im Vorfeld vorauszusehen.
Frage dich, was dein Gegenüber evtl. nicht oder anders verstehen könnte und erkläre diese Stellen besonders genau und evtl. auf unterschiedliche Arten.

SF 18 Agreeing and disagreeing with people's opinions ➜ *SB (p. 134)*

LANGUAGE HELP: Es ist bei Diskussionen hilfreich, einige Standard-Redewendungen parat zu haben. Wenn du die beherrschst, kannst du dich mehr auf deine Argumente konzentrieren. Folgende Phrasen solltest du dir aufschreiben und sie lernen:

Stating your opinion	Agreeing	Disagreeing
• *In my opinion …*	• *I agree …*	• *I'm afraid I don't quite agree …*
• *Well, I'd say …*	• *Exactly./Absolutely./…*	• *I'm not sure about that.*
• *It's a fact that …*	• *You're quite right.*	• *Do you really think so?*
• *Personally, I think…*	• *I think so too.*	• *I'm not convinced that …*
• *If you ask me …*	• *You've got a good point there.*	• *I doubt that (very much).*
• *I think/feel/believe …*	• *That's exactly how I see it.*	• *I don't agree with you at all.*
• *First of all, I'd like to point out…*	• *That's true/right.*	• *I disagree (completely).*
• *I'm certain that …*	• *I couldn't agree with you more.*	• *It's not as simple as that.*

SF 22 Listening strategies ➜ *SB (pp. 139–140)*

Hörverstehenstechniken

Es gibt zwei verschiedene Herangehensweisen:

- **Top-down-Technik:**
  das Verstehen beginnt von der Gesprächssituation her:
  Beim Hören eines englischen Textes hilft es, sich bewusst zu werden über den Kontext, den Sprecher und seine Rolle, wie gesprochen wird (Emotion, Tempo, Sprachebene, …) und was dabei das Thema ist.
  Solche Informationen helfen dir oft mit einiger Treffsicherheit zu erraten, was im Gespräch gemeint ist, selbst wenn du nicht jedes gesprochene Wort verstehst.
- **Bottom-up-Technik:**
  die Erschließung der Bedeutung beginnt beim Gesprochenen selbst:
  Die Dekodierung der Laute, die du in der Fremdsprache hörst, ist eine Frage der Übung. Achte möglichst genau darauf, was gerade gesagt wird und beachte dabei z. B. die Besonderheiten verschiedener Akzente.
- **Chunks:**
  Im Englischen spricht man oft mehrere Wörter als Einheit aus, bei der Wortgrenzen verschwinden. Das findet man verstärkt bei
  - Ausdrücken mit Modalverben: *she'd've told me* • *you shouldn't've bought it* • *you mustabin asleep*
  - häufigen Alltagsphrasen: *Whatcha think o'that?* • *Howdju feel?* • *Dincha see it?*
  - Wörter, die gesprochen gleich klingen, sich in der Bedeutung aber unterscheiden:
    We'd like ice in our drinks. – We like ice in our drinks.
    I can't see them now. – I can see them now. (besonders im AE)
    Hier schafft im Gespräch gezieltes Nachfragen Sicherheit:
    Sorry, was that can or can't?

TIPP: Es gibt dir Sicherheit, wenn du dich von vornherein auf **typische Missverständnisse durch Akzente** einstellst.
Versuche, dir folgende Beispiele mal mit britischem und dann mit amerikanischem oder australischem Akzent vorzustellen: *can't* • *stop* • *pretty* • *student* • *main* • *text* • *tea*

TIPP: Um sich auf die **Chunks** im Gespräch einzustimmen, kannst du die häufigsten Wendungen, die beim Sprechen verkürzt ausgesprochen werden, einmal in voller Länge aufschreiben.

Anforderungen an das Hörverstehen

Listening for detail

- Überleg dir vorher, auf welche Informationen du achten musst.
  - Bei einem Wetterbericht sind das z. B. Beschreibungen wie *sunny, cloudy, chance of rain* etc., bei Bahnhofsansagen z. B. Wörter wie *platform* oder Orte und Zeiten.
  - Höre dann gezielt auf solche Wörter und notiere sie.
- Manchmal können auch Signalwörter helfen, dem Inhalt zu folgen und dich auf die Details zu konzentrieren:
  - Gründe, Folgen: *because, so, so that, …*
  - Vergleiche: *larger/older/… than, as … as, more, most, …*
  - Reihenfolge: *before, after, then, next, later, …*

Listening for gist

- Mache dir keine Sorgen, wenn du nicht jedes Wort verstehst – das brauchst du nicht, um der Grundaussage folgen zu können. Überlege dir vorher, um was es gehen könnte (z. B. anhand des Themas) und konzentriere dich darauf.
- Versuche, von den Sachen, die du verstehst, auf Inhalte zu schließen, die noch kommen könnten.

TIPP:
- Oft kannst du die Menschen um dich herum fragen, wenn du nicht alles richtig verstanden hast – z. B. bei Durchsagen am Bahnhof.
- In einer Unterhaltung kannst du deinen Gesprächspartner bitten, Sachen zu wiederholen oder zu erklären.

TIPP: Im **Unterricht** kannst du Texte oft zweimal hören und hast weitere Hilfen:
- Sieh dir die Aufgabenstellung an: Was sollst du heraushören?
- Sieh dir Titel und Bilder an.
- Vergleiche nach dem Hören mit einem Partner, was ihr verstanden habt.
- Vervollständige deine Notizen sofort.

SF 24 Giving a presentation ➔ SB (p. 141)

Vorbereitung der Präsentation

Step 1: **Recherchiere** dein Thema (➔ *SF 28*) und mach dir Notizen, am besten gleich auf Englisch.

Step 2: **Strukturiere** die Informationen, z. B. mit einer Gliederung. (➔ *SF 6*)

Step 3: Wähle eine **Form der Präsentation** aus, die das Thema gut veranschaulicht (Poster, Folie, …). Gestalte dein Poster/deine Folie und beachte dabei die Grundsätze für ein gutes Poster.

Step 4: Bereite deine **Notizen** für die Präsentation vor, z. B. auf nummerierten Karteikarten. Verwende keine ganzen Sätze, sondern Stichworte, Symbole oder Halbsätze. Notiere dir z. B. auch schwierige Wörter und ihre Aussprache.

Step 5: Wenn du in einem Team arbeitest, entscheidet gemeinsam, wer welchen Teil der Präsentation übernimmt.

Step 6: **Übe deine Präsentation** zu Hause vor einem Spiegel oder vor einem kleinen Publikum (Eltern, Großeltern, Freunde).

TIPP: Um ein **gutes Poster** zu gestalten, solltest du folgendes beachten:
- Wähle eine passende Überschrift.
- Schreibe groß und für alle gut lesbar.
- Ergänze passende Bilder, um den Text/die Inhalte zu veranschaulichen.

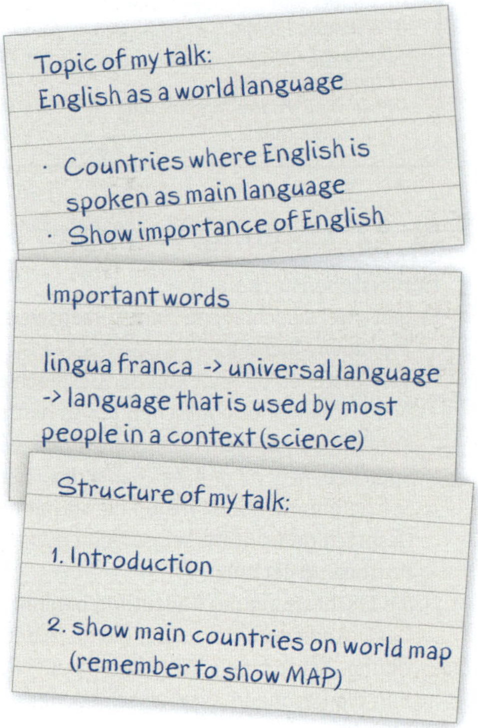

Halten der Präsentation

Step 1: **Warte, bis es ruhig ist**. Schau die Zuhörer/innen an. Erkläre, worüber du sprechen wirst und wie deine Präsentation aufgebaut ist.

Step 2: **Sprich langsam** und deutlich und möglichst frei. Lies nicht von deinen Notizen ab.

Step 3: Beende deine Präsentation mit einer kleinen **Zusammenfassung** der wichtigsten Punkte. Bedanke dich fürs Zuhören und beantworte Fragen zu deinem Vortrag.

My presentation is about … First I'd like to talk about …

Here's a new word. It is … in German.

On my poster you can see a photo of … The mind map shows …

Thank you for listening. Do you have any questions?

SF 25 Describing and interpreting images ➔ SB (p. 142)

Beschreibung

Step 1: Stelle das Bild vor und sage, woher es kommt.

Step 2: Beschreibe das Bild:
- Sage, was wo zu sehen ist: *at the top/bottom* · *in the foreground/background* · *in the middle* · *on the left/right*
- Geh bei der Beschreibung in einer bestimmten Reihenfolge vor, z. B. von links nach rechts oder von oben nach unten.
- Diese Präpositionen sind auch hilfreich: *behind* · *between* · *in front of* · *next to* · *under* · *above*
- Beziehe dich – v. a. bei Cartoons – auch auf Bildunterschriften,- Sprechblasen, etc.: *The caption reads …* · *One of the characters says/thinks …*

1 *I'd like to talk about this photo of …/ cartoon …/I found it online/ in a magazine/…*

2 *In the foreground you can see … I think the people in the photo/ cartoon are talking about …*

3 *I really like/don't like the photo/cartoon because … It's interesting/boring/ … because …*

4 *Thank you for listening. Do you have any questions?*

Interpretation

Step 1: Sage, was deiner Meinung nach die Botschaft des Bildes/Cartoons ist:
- *This is a political/environmental/educational/… photo/cartoon.*
- *I think the message is …*
- *It's about …*
- *… shows that …*
- *The fact that there is … means …*
- *The picture/cartoon may be meant to show …*

Step 2: Sage, weshalb du das Bild/den Cartoon wirksam/witzig findest (oder nicht):
- *The picture/cartoon clearly shows …*
- *The message is made clear by showing/saying …*
- *I really laughed at the cartoon because it …*
- *I don't find the cartoon funny because …*
- *The picture/cartoon speaks to us directly by …*

Wenn du das Bild/den Cartoon in einer Präsentation vorstellst, musst du evtl. genauer erklären, weshalb du es/ihn ausgewählt hast oder was daran witzig ist:
- *I chose this picture because …*
- *The joke is that …*
- *It's funny because …*
- *The picture/cartoon is criticizing/making fun of …*

"Now don't forget to go on social media and rate today's lesson plan."

SF 26 Talking about statistics ➔ *SB (p. 143)*

Statistiken können auf unterschiedliche Weise dargestellt werden: Tortendiagramm **(pie chart)**, Säulendiagramm **(bar chart)**, Kurvendiagramm **(line graph)** oder in einer Tabelle **(table)**. Wenn du Statistiken analysieren und vorstellen sollst, gehst du am besten wie folgt vor:

Step 1: Identifiziere, welche Art von Diagramm du vor dir hast – **pie chart**, **bar chart**, **line graph** oder Tabelle – und sieh dir die Quelle an:
- Ist die Quelle verlässlich?
  Ist der Herausgeber z. B. ein Ministerium/eine Behörde oder eine Organisation wie *amnesty international*?
- Sind die Angaben/Zahlen im Diagramm aktuell?
  Wenn du z. B. eine Statistik zu Kinderarmut in Großbritannien vor dir hast, ist es ein wichtiger Unterschied, ob die Zahlen von 1973 oder 2013 sind.

Step 2: Beschreibe das Diagramm/die Tabelle:
- Worum geht es? Welche Informationen gibt das Diagramm?
  The bar chart/pie chart/line graph/table … shows the different …/ compares the size/number of …/is about …/contrasts … with …
- Zeigen die Daten eine Entwicklung oder werden verschiedene Zeitpunkte miteinander verglichen?
  It shows … in contrast to …
  The chart gives us information about who/what/how many/…
- Werden absolute Zahlen oder Prozentangaben verwendet?
  The chart/table shows us the number of/percentage of …
  It shows which percentage of …

Step 3: Ziehe deine Schlussfolgerungen aus dem Diagramm/der Tabelle:
My main conclusion is that …
The most imporant thing I've learned is that …
One thing that I hadn't realized before is …

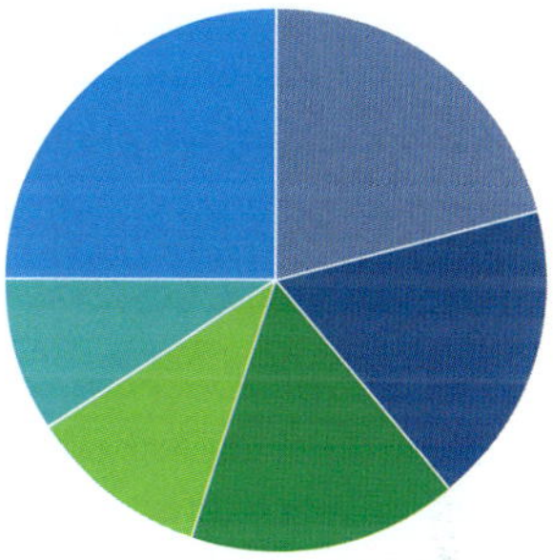

pie chart

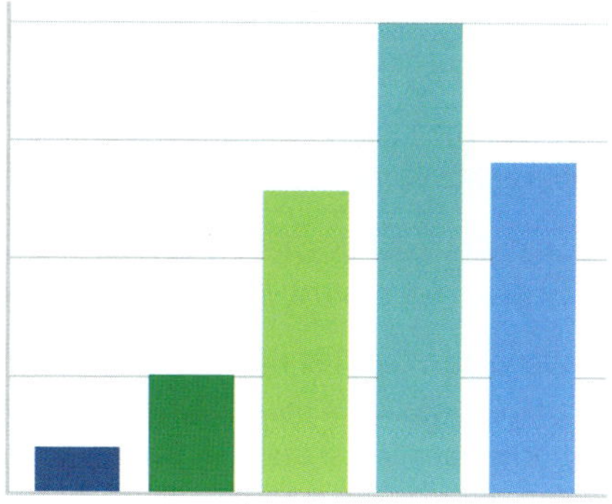

bar chart

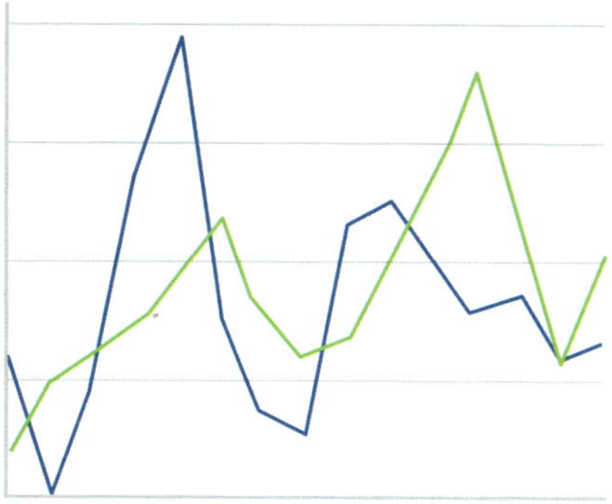

line graph

LANGUAGE HELP:
Wenn du über Diagramme sprichst, können dir folgende Redewendungen helfen:

Pie chart
- *The pie chart is divided into … segments, which show/represent …*
- *The smallest/biggest segment …*
- *The segments representing … and … constitute the majority …*
- *A huge majority/minority is …*

Bar chart
- *The bars are arranged horizontally/vertically.*
- *There are big/vast/surprising differences between …*
- *At the top/bottom of the ranking comes …*
- *… is first/last in rank.*
- *… has the largest/second largest …*

Line graph
- *The graph shows the relationship between … and …*
- *… is twice/three times as high as …*
- *There are more than/nearly twice as many … as there are …*
- *… increase/decrease/reach a high point/rise/fall/drop/grow steadily*

SF 28 Internet research (Finding information for a presentation) ➜ *SB (p. 144)*

Step 1: Überlege dir gute **Stichwörter** für dein Thema und gib sie in eine **Suchmaschine** ein. Je besser die Suchbegriffe sind, desto genauer sind die Ergebnisse. Die Infografik rechts hilft dir, wenn du ganz spezielle Informationen suchst.

Step 2: Nutze die **Erweiterte Suche**. Dort kannst du nicht nur festlegen, in welcher Sprache deine Ergebnisse sein sollen, sondern auch das Land eingrenzen (z. B. nur Ergebnisse aus den USA) oder die Domäne (z. B. .edu, .gov, .org).

Step 3: Sieh dir mehrere **Suchergebnisse** an, um zu sehen, ob sie passen (➜ *SF 1*).

Step 4: Achte darauf, wer die Webseite erstellt hat, um die **Qualität** der Suchergebnisse einzuschätzen.

Step 5: Speichere die besten Ergebnisse als Lesezeichen ab, damit du schnell darauf zugreifen kannst. Ordne deine Lesezeichen thematisch zur besseren Übersichtlichkeit.

Step 6: Setz dir ein **Zeitlimit** für deine Recherche und ordne dann dein Material. Prüfe, ob etwas fehlt, und suche dann ggf. gezielt nach diesen Informationen.

Step 7: Wenn du einen Text oder eine Präsentation vorbereitest, kopiere nicht einfach Inhalte von Webseiten. Mach dir **Notizen** und verwende deine eigenen Worte, um die Inhalte wiederzugeben.

Internet research
Tipps und Tricks

Wenn du ganz spezifische Informationen suchst, helfen diese Tricks:

Was du suchst: Artikel aus dem *Guardian* von 2000–2014 über den Liverpool FC in der Champions League.

Wie du danach suchst:

site:theguardian.com "Liverpool FC" "champions league" 2000..2014

site:	" "	..
sucht nur auf der genannten Seite	sucht den exakten Begriff	zeigt nur Ergebnisse aus diesem Zeitraum

Was du suchst: Einen englischsprachigen Bericht, am liebsten als PDF, über den Lebensraum von Füchsen.

Wie du danach suchst:

filetype:pdf intitle:habitat of *fox

filetype:	intitle:	*
sucht nur diesen Dateityp (pdf, doc, jpg usw.)	zeigt nur Ergebnisse, in denen dieses Wort im Titel auftaucht	sucht auch Worte wie Red Fox, Black Fox, Desert Fox usw.

SF 29 Dealing with unknown words ➜ *SB (p. 145)*

Nachschlagen kostet Zeit und ist nicht immer nötig. Diese Tipps können dir helfen, unbekannte Wörter auch ohne ein Wörterbuch zu erschließen:

- Sieh dir die Überschrift, die Zwischenüberschriften und Bilder sowie den **Kontext** an. Beispiel: *Let's hurry. The train* ***departs*** *in ten minutes.*
- Wenn du einen **Teil des Wortes** kennst, kannst du oft die Bedeutung erschließen, z. B. *knowledge = things someone knows*
  bottle opener = something you use to open bottles
- Viele englische Wörter haben eine **Ähnlichkeit** zu deutschen Wörtern (z. B. *brochure, statue, insect*) oder Wörtern aus anderen Sprachen, z. B. *voice* (*French: voix; Latin: vox*).

TIPP: Nicht alle Wörter, die im Deutschen und Englischen ähnlich sind, haben auch dieselbe Bedeutung.
Achte daher auf **false friends**:
handy = praktisch, nicht Handy

GF 1 The tenses ➔ SB (pp. 149–154)

1.2 Talking about the present

The simple present

*At home, Leon **usually** **gets** the bus to school.*
***On Fridays** his mother **takes** him in the car.*
*He **never** **cycles** to school because it's too far.*

Das ***simple present*** wird verwendet,

- um über Handlungen und Ereignisse zu sprechen, die **wiederholt, regelmäßig, immer** oder **nie** geschehen. Signalwörter für das *simple present* sind Zeitangaben wie *always, usually, often, every week, on Fridays, never* u. Ä.

*Olivia Wilson and her family **live** in Nottingham.*
*Her mum is Italian, so she **speaks** two languages.*
*She **plays** hockey and **collects** old computer games.*
*Her parents **work** for a computer company.*

- um über **Dauerzustände** sowie über **Hobbys** und **Berufe** zu sprechen.

The present progressive

*What**'s** Mr Bennett **doing**?*
*He's **making** a salad.*

Das ***present progressive*** wird verwendet,

- um über Handlungen und Ereignisse zu sprechen, die **jetzt gerade** im Gange sind. Signalwörter für das *present progressive* sind *at the moment, now, just*.

Mr Bennett (on the phone):
*"I'**m** **making** a salad."* — *"I'm busy, Jack. I'**m making** a salad."*

! Die Handlung, um die es geht, kann für einen Augenblick unterbrochen sein, z. B. durch ein Telefonat.
Wichtig ist, dass sie noch nicht abgeschlossen ist.

*Olivia has got a holiday job: she**'s working** as a waitress in a small café in Devon. She**'s sharing** a room with another waitress while she's there.*

- um über **vorübergehende Zustände** zu sprechen (begrenzter Zeitraum: *while she's there*).

1.3 Talking about the past

The simple past

***Twenty years ago**, Olivia's mother **moved** to England.*
Vor zwanzig Jahren ist Olivias Mutter nach England gezogen/zog Olivias Mutter nach England.

***Last Friday** Olivia's family **flew** to Italy.*

Das ***simple past*** wird verwendet,

- um über **abgeschlossene** Handlungen und Ereignisse zu sprechen, die zu **einem bestimmten Zeitpunkt in der Vergangenheit** stattfanden. Signalwörter für das *simple past* sind genaue Zeitangaben wie *twenty years ago, last Friday, yesterday, in 2012* u. Ä.

*Yesterday Olivia **went** to town with a friend.*
*First they **looked** round the shops, and Katie **bought** a CD.*
*Then they **tried** on shoes in four shops, but they **didn't buy** any. After that they **had** an ice cream.*

- wenn man über vergangene Ereignisse berichtet oder eine Geschichte erzählt (oft mit *first …, then …, after that …*).

! Im Deutschen steht oft das Perfekt, wo im Englischen das *simple past* stehen muss.

„Früher …" – *used to* + infinitive/*would* + infinitive

*We **used to live** in Manchester.*
Wir wohnten früher in Manchester.
*Manchester United **used to be** my favourite team.*
Früher war Manchester United meine Lieblingsmannschaft.
*I **used to spend** lots of money on sports magazines.*
Ich habe früher immer viel Geld für Sportzeitschriften ausgegeben.

Wenn man beschreiben will, was **früher der Fall war**, aber heute nicht mehr, dann kann man die Konstruktion ***used to* + Infinitiv** verwenden.

*Grandpa **would visit** us every Sunday after church.*
Opa besuchte uns jeden Sonntag nach der Kirche./
Opa pflegte uns jeden Sonntag nach der Kirche zu besuchen.

Zum Ausdruck von **früher gewohnheitsmäßig wiederholten Handlungen** wird auch ***would* + *Infinitiv*** verwendet.

The past progressive

Yesterday at 3.30 Olivia ***was walking*** *home from school.*
It ***was raining****, so lots of people* ***were hurrying*** *to the bus stop.*

Sally ***was cycling*** *home when a dog* ***ran*** *out in front of her bike.*
Sally radelte (gerade) nach Hause, als ihr ein Hund vors Fahrrad lief.

Das ***past progressive*** wird verwendet,

- um über Handlungen und Ereignisse zu sprechen, die **zu einem bestimmten Zeitpunkt in der Vergangenheit** noch im Gange, also **noch nicht abgeschlossen** waren.
- wenn man beschreiben will, was gerade vor sich ging *(she was cycling home)*, als etwas anderes passierte *(a dog ran out in front of her bike)*.

The past perfect (simple)

When Emily arrived at the diner, her parents ***had*** *already* ***eaten****.*
Als Emily im Restaurant ankam, hatten ihre Eltern schon gegessen.

Grandpa ***had*** *already* ***been*** *in hospital for a week when we returned from Spain.*
Opa lag schon eine Woche im Krankenhaus, als wir aus Spanien zurückkehrten.

Das ***past perfect*** wird verwendet,

- um auszudrücken, dass eine Handlung noch **vor einer anderen Handlung in der Vergangenheit** stattgefunden hatte.
- um auszudrücken, dass ein Zustand noch **vor einem Zeitpunkt in der Vergangenheit** begonnen hatte.

The past perfect progressive

Olivia was very tired when she arrived home.
She ***had been studying*** *for a test all day.*
… Sie hatte den ganzen Tag für einen Test gelernt.

We ***had been playing*** *tennis for half an hour when it started to rain.*
Wir hatten eine halbe Stunde Tennis gespielt, als es anfing zu regnen.

Das ***past perfect progressive*** wird verwendet, um auszudrücken, dass eine Handlung vor einem Zeitpunkt in der Vergangenheit begonnen hatte und bis (oder fast bis) zu jenem Zeitpunkt andauerte.

1.4 Talking about the past and the present

Present perfect und ***present perfect progressive*** haben mit der Vergangenheit und mit der Gegenwart zu tun.

The present perfect (simple)

1 *Matt Damon is great. I****'ve seen*** *all his films.*
2 *My sister loves books about horses. She****'s read*** *hundreds of them.*
3 *Mel* ***has lost*** *her mobile. Now she can't phone her friends and her mum is angry.*
4 *I****'ve bought*** *some new jeans, look. They'll go well with my red top.*
5 *Luke* ***has already done*** *his Maths homework, but he* ***hasn't started*** *his French* ***yet****.*
6 *I****'ve never been*** *to Paris.* ***Have*** *you* ***ever been*** *there?*
– No, I ***haven't****. But I****'ve always wanted*** *to go.*

Das ***present perfect*** wird verwendet,

- um über Handlungen und Ereignisse zu sprechen, die **irgendwann in der Vergangenheit** geschehen sind.

Wie in den Sätzen **3** und **4** hat das Geschehen oft **Auswirkungen auf die Gegenwart oder die Zukunft**.

Ein genauer Zeitpunkt wird nicht genannt. Häufig werden jedoch Adverbien der unbestimmten Zeit wie *already, always, just, not … yet, often, never* in *present perfect*-Sätzen verwendet – wie in den Sätzen **5** und **6**.

Leon ***has been*** *a member of his football club* ***for*** *ten years now/****since*** *his sixth birthday.*
Leon ist jetzt seit zehn Jahren/seit seinem sechsten Geburtstag Mitglied in seinem Fußballverein.

- um über **Zustände** zu sprechen, die in der Vergangenheit begonnen haben und jetzt noch andauern – oft mit *since* bzw. *for* = deutsch „seit".

! Im Deutschen benutzt man in diesen Fällen meist das Präsens, aber im Englischen **muss** das *present perfect* stehen:
Ich kenne ihn seit … *I've known him since/for …*

Zustandsverben sind z. B. *be, have, know, like, hate*.

> *„seit …" – since/for*
>
> ***since*** **+ Zeitpunkt** (wann etwas begann)
> ***We've had*** *our dog* ***since April****.*
> … seit April
>
> ***for*** **+ Zeitraum** (wie lange etwas andauert)
> *We****'ve had*** *our dog* ***for three months****.*
> … seit drei Monaten

The present perfect progressive

1 *She**'s been writing** letters all afternoon.*
Sie schreibt (schon) den ganzen Nachmittag Briefe.

2 *My brother **has been playing** the piano since 2013.*
Mein Bruder spielt seit 2013 Klavier.

3 *I**'ve been learning** French for three years now.*
Ich lerne jetzt seit drei Jahren Französisch.

Das ***present perfect progressive*** wird verwendet, um auszudrücken, dass eine **Handlung in der Vergangenheit begonnen** hat und jetzt **noch andauert** (auch wenn die Handlung nicht ununterbrochen im Gange war wie etwa in den Sätzen **2** und **3**).

! Auch in diesen Fällen verwenden wir im Deutschen meist das Präsens: *Er spielt seit …*
Aber im Englischen steht das *present perfect progressive*: *He's been playing … since/for …*

1.5 Talking about the future

The *will*-future

*I**'ll be** 15 next October.*
*It **will be** cold and windy, and we **will get** some rain in the afternoon.*

*I suppose Ella **will be** late again as usual.*
Ich nehme an, Ella kommt wie üblich wieder zu spät.

NEW *Just a moment. I**'ll open** the door for you.*
Moment. Ich mache Ihnen die Tür auf.

*I **won't tell** anyone what's happened. I promise.*
Ich sage niemandem, was passiert ist. …

Das ***will-future*** wird verwendet,

- um **Vorhersagen** über die Zukunft zu äußern. Oft geht es dabei um Dinge, die man nicht beeinflussen kann, z. B. das Alter oder das Wetter.
- um eine **Vermutung** auszudrücken (oft eingeleitet mit *I suppose, I think, I'm sure, I expect, maybe*).
- wenn man sich **spontan** – also ohne es im Voraus geplant zu haben – zu etwas entschließt. Oft geht es dabei um **Hilfsangebote** oder **Versprechen**.

The *going to*-future

*After school I**'m going to study** architecture.*
Nach der Schule werde ich Architektur studieren/habe ich vor, Architektur zu studieren.

*The Millers **are going to move** to New Zealand.*
Die Millers werden/wollen nach Neuseeland ziehen.

NEW *Look at those clouds. There**'s going to be** a storm.*
… Es wird ein Gewitter geben.

*Oh dear! Your mother**'s going to be** very angry with us.*
… Deine Mutter wird sehr wütend auf uns sein.

Das ***going to-future*** wird verwendet,

- um über **Vorhaben** zu sprechen, zu denen man sich schon vor einiger Zeit entschlossen hat (also über Dinge, die man bereits **geplant** hat).
- um zu betonen, dass man ganz sicher ist, dass etwas gleich geschehen wird (meist gibt es bereits deutliche **Anzeichen** dafür).

The present progressive (with future meaning)

*We**'re driving** to Scotland next weekend to visit my grandparents.*
*I**'m meeting** a friend in town tomorrow at 12.*
*All my friends **are coming** to my birthday party on Friday.*

Wenn etwas für die Zukunft **fest verabredet** ist, kann man auch das ***present progressive*** verwenden. Es muss aber deutlich sein, dass es sich um etwas Zukünftiges handelt, z. B. durch eine Zeitangabe *(next weekend, tomorrow, on Sunday)* oder aus dem Zusammenhang.

(Man nennt diese Verwendung des *present progressive* manchmal ***diary future***, weil es dabei oft um Verabredungen geht, die schon im Terminkalender eingetragen sind.)

The simple present (with future meaning)

*Our cookery classes **start** on 2 September.*
*The film **starts** at 8 o'clock.*
*When **does** the next train to Liverpool **leave**?*
*The club **meets** in an hour, so we'll have to hurry.*

Das ***simple present*** mit futurischer Bedeutung wird verwendet, wenn ein zukünftiges Geschehen durch einen **Fahrplan**, ein **Programm** oder Ähnliches genau festgelegt ist. Verben wie ***arrive, leave, go, open, close, start, stop*** werden häufig so verwendet.

(Diese Verwendung des *simple present* wird als ***timetable future*** bezeichnet.)

Wenn man im Englischen über Zukünftiges sprechen will, dann spielen bei der Wahl der richtigen Zeitform die Begriffe ***decision* (Entscheidung, Beschluss), *prediction* (Vorhersage)** und ***arrangement* (Vereinbarung)** eine entscheidende Rolle. Die folgende Tabelle kann dir helfen, die richtige Entscheidung zu treffen.

	will-future	*going to*-future	present progressive	simple present
Decision (Entscheidung)	spontane Entscheidung	im Voraus geplant		
Prediction (Vorhersage)	Vermutungen und Vorhersagen	betont sichere Vorhersage (Anzeichen vorhanden)		
Arrangement (Vereinbarung)		seltener, aber nicht falsch	fest verabredet ("diary future")	Fahrplan, Programm ("timetable future")

The future progressive

*This time next week my sister will be on her way to Spain – and I'**ll be doing** my maths exam.*
Nächste Woche um diese Zeit wird meine Schwester auf dem Weg nach Spanien sein – und ich werde dabei sein, meine Mathe-Prüfung zu machen.

*What **will** you **be doing** over the next couple of days?*

*How long **will** you **be staying** in Washington?*

***Will** you **be staying** for dinner?*

Das ***future progressive*** beschreibt Handlungen und Ereignisse, die **in der Zukunft im Gange sein werden** (noch nicht abgeschlossen sein werden).
Typische Zeitangaben sind *a week today* („heute in einer Woche"), *this time next week* und Ähnliches.

Das ***future progressive*** wird oft verwendet, um sich höflich nach den Plänen anderer zu erkundigen.

The future perfect

***Next Friday** we **will have finished** all our exams.*
Nächsten Freitag werden wir alle unsere Prüfungen geschafft haben.

*And **by the end of next week** we'**ll have received** our results.*
Und bis Ende nächster Woche werden wir unsere Ergebnisse erhalten haben.

Das ***future perfect*** wird verwendet um auszudrücken, dass etwas **in der Zukunft geschehen oder getan sein wird**. (Meist wird ein Zeitpunkt genannt – hier: *next Friday; by the end of next week.*)

GF 2 Aspect: the simple form and the progressive form → *SB (pp. 154–155)*

2.1 Simple and progressive form in contrast

Tense	Simple form	Progressive form
Present tense	sing(s)	am/are/is singing
Past tense	sang	was/were singing
Present perfect	have/has sung	have/has been singing
Past percfect	had sung	had been singing
will-future	will sing	will be singing

Anders als im Deutschen gibt es im Englischen eine **einfache Form** *(simple form)* und eine **Verlaufsform** *(progressive form)* des Verbs.

Mit diesen Formen bringt man zum Ausdruck,
- ob eine Handlung regelmäßig oder wiederholt stattfindet **oder** ob sie sich gerade im Verlauf befindet,
- ob eine Handlung abgeschlossen ist **oder** ob sie noch andauert.

1 *Tom **works** at a garage on Saturdays.* (regelmäßig)
2 *Mr Clark **goes** to work by bike.* (immer, jeden Tag)
3 *Lucy **has written** three letters today.* (sie ist fertig)

4 *Tom isn't in. He'**s working**.* (jetzt gerade)
5 *This week Mr Clark **is going** by bus.* (nur diese Woche, denn sein Rad ist kaputt)
6 *Lucy **has been writing** letters all day.* (sie ist noch dabei)

Die ***simple form*** wird verwendet
- für regelmäßige/wiederholte Handlungen (**1**)
- für Dauerzustände (wenn etwas immer so ist) (**2**)
- für abgeschlossene Handlungen (**3**).

Die ***progressive form*** wird verwendet
- für Handlungen, die gerade im Verlauf sind (**4**)
- für vorübergehende Zustände (wenn etwas nur vorübergehend der Fall ist) (**5**)
- für Handlungen, die noch nicht abgeschlossen sind (**6**).

2.2 Activity verbs

(in a shop window)	*We **make** the best pizza in town!*
(on the phone)	*Carol **is making** a pizza. Can she call you back?*

*It **gets** dark very early here in winter.*
*At 5 o'clock it **was** already **getting** dark.*

Tätigkeitsverben *(activity verbs)* bezeichnen **Tätigkeiten** *(do, go, make, read, …)* oder **Vorgänge** *(become, get, rain, …)*.

Sie können sowohl in der ***simple form*** als auch in der ***progressive form*** verwendet werden.

2.3 State verbs

*The price **doesn't include** breakfast.*
*Emily **seems** really happy at her new school.*
*Jake's uncle **owns** a nice house in the country.*

***Do** you **believe** their story?*
*I **don't know** the answer to question 5.*
*Anna **didn't understand** what Julie **meant**.*

*Lucy **doesn't like** people who talk a lot.*
*I **don't mind** waiting for you here.*
*We **prefer** brown bread to white bread. It's healthier.*

Zustandsverben *(state verbs)* bezeichnen keine Tätigkeiten oder Vorgänge, sondern **Zustände**. Sie werden in der Regel nur in der ***simple form*** verwendet.

Zu den **Zustandsverben** gehören

- Verben, die **Eigenschaften**, **Besitz** oder **Zugehörigkeit** ausdrücken, z. B. *be, exist, include, seem, sound, mean* („bedeuten"), *cost, need, own, belong, …*
- Verben des **Meinens** und des **Wissens**, z. B. *believe, know, mean* („meinen"), *remember, imagine, realize, recognize, understand, …*
- Verben des **Mögens** und **Wollens**, z. B. *like, love, dislike, hate, mind, prefer, want, …*

States and activities

*Julie **has** dark hair.*	**state:**	„haben"
*Julie **is having** a shower.*	**activity:**	„duschen"
*We **were having** fun/a great time.*	**activity:**	„Spaß/eine tolle Zeit haben"
***Do** I **look** silly with my hair like this?*	**state:**	„aussehen"
*I didn't see him. I **wasn't looking**.*	**activity:**	„(hin)schauen, gucken"
*The flowers **smell** wonderful.*	**state:**	„riechen"
*Sophie **is smelling** the roses.*	**activity:**	„an etwas riechen"
*The pizza **tastes** good.*	**state:**	„schmecken"
***I'm tasting** the soup now.*	**activity:**	„kosten, probieren"
*I **think** that's a great idea.*	**state:**	„denken, meinen"
*He **was thinking** of moving to Paris.*	**activity:**	„überlegen, nachdenken"

Einige wenige englische Verben können als **Tätigkeits- oder als Zustandsverb** verwendet werden (mit jeweils unterschiedlichen deutschen Entsprechungen).

Als **Zustandsverb** stehen diese Verben immer in der ***simple form***.

Als **Tätigkeitsverb** kommen sie in beiden Formen vor.

Vergleiche die Beispiele im Kasten links.

GF 3 The passive ➜ *SB (pp. 156–158)*

3.2 The passive: use

1 *The first goal **was scored** in the seventh minute.*
… wurde erzielt …

2 *A new sports centre **has been opened** in Paddington.*
… ist eröffnet worden …

3 *Breakfast **is served** from 7 to 10.30 am.*
… wird serviert …

4 *The bank robbers **have been sentenced** to ten years.*
… sind verurteilt worden …

*The driver **was questioned by** the police.*
Der Fahrer wurde von der Polizei verhört/befragt.

Mit einem **Passivsatz** kann man Handlungen beschreiben, ohne zu sagen, wer die Handlung ausführt.

Oft ist nicht bekannt oder dem Sprecher nicht wichtig, wer die Handlung ausführt (Sätze **1** und **2**), manchmal ist es auch offensichtlich und daher nicht erwähnenswert (Sätze **3** und **4**).

Wenn man in einem Passivsatz „Täter" oder „Verursacher" nennen will, kann man die Präposition ***by*** verwenden.

3.3 The passive: form

States and activities	
Simple present	*English **is spoken** in lots of countries.*
Simple past	*The bridge **was completed** in 1998.*
Present perfect	*All the biscuits **have been eaten**.*
Past perfect	*I didn't go to the party because I **hadn't been invited**.*
***going to*-future**	*Look, the lions **are going to be fed** soon.*
***will*-future and modal auxiliaries**	*The last match of the season **will be played** next Friday.* *Mobile phones **should be turned off** during lessons.* *Concert tickets **can be bought** online.*
Future perfect	*I'm sure lots of new planets **will have been discovered** by 2050.*
Present progressive	*Three new blocks of flats **are being built** in King Street.*
Past progressive	*The museum was closed. The rooms **were being painted**.*

Das Passiv bildet man mit einer **Form von *be*** und der **3. Form des Verbs** (Partizip Perfekt, *past participle*).

➜ *Unregelmäßige Verben: SB, S. 240–241*

Bei den *progressive forms* wird das Passiv mit *being* gebildet: *are being built; were being painted*.

*A boy **got hurt** yesterday when he was hit by a car.*

*John's parents **got killed** in a fire when he was 12.*

In informellem Englisch wird statt einer Form von *be* manchmal eine **Form von *get* zur Passivbildung** verwendet, vor allem bei kurzen Vorgängen, die plötzlich und unerwartet eintreten (wie z. B. Unfälle).

GF 4 Modals and their substitutes ➜ *SB (pp. 158–161)*

4.1 Modal auxiliaries

can, may, must, should sind modale Hilfsverben.
Sie drücken aus, was jemand tun **kann, darf, muss, soll** usw.
Sie werden zusammen mit dem Infinitiv eines Vollverbs verwendet (**1**).
Nur in Kurzantworten können sie allein stehen (**2**).

1 ***Can** you **play** the piano?*
2 *– Yes, I **can**./No, I **can't**.*

Weitere Merkmale modaler Hilfsverben:
- Sie haben **nur eine Form**, es gibt also keine Endungen auf *-s, -ing* oder *-ed* (**3**).
- Frage und Verneinung werden **ohne** *do/does/did* gebildet (**4**).
- Sie beziehen sich in der Regel auf die Gegenwart oder die Zukunft (**5, 6**).

3 *She's so good at drawing. She **should** study art.*

4 ***Could** you **do** the exercise? – No, I **couldn't**.*
5 ***Can** we help you in the kitchen, Mum?*
6 *We **can** play tennis on Saturday if you like.*

4.2 Substitutes

1 *I'd love **to be able to** play the piano.*
Ich würde liebend gern Klavier spielen können.

2 ***Being able to** play the piano must be great.*
Es muss großartig sein, Klavier spielen zu können.

3 *We **weren't allowed to** use dictionaries in the test.*
Wir durften im Test keine Wörterbücher benutzen.

Modale Hilfsverben können nicht alle Zeitformen bilden. Daher gibt es zu bestimmten modalen Hilfsverben Ersatzverben mit ähnlicher Bedeutung, von denen man
- den Infinitiv (**1**),
- die *-ing*-Form (**2**),
- alle Zeitformen (**3**, hier: *simple past*)

bilden kann.

Sieh dir die Beispielsätze für deutsch **„können"**, **„dürfen"** und **„müssen"** im Folgenden an.

„können" –
can/(to) be able to

*My little brother **can/is able to** swim.*

present: can und *am/is/are able to*

*Tim **could/was able to** read when he was four.*
*I **could** smell fire, but I **couldn't** see any smoke.*

past: could und *was/were able to*
(*could* steht vor allem in verneinten Sätzen und Fragen und mit Verben der Wahrnehmung wie *smell, see, hear*.)

*I **haven't been able to** contact him yet.*

present perfect: have/has been able to

*I'm taking driving lessons, so next year I'**ll be able to** drive.*

will-future: will be able to

**„dürfen" –
can, may/(to) be allowed to**

Can/May *I have a sleepover on Friday, Mum?* *We* ***aren't allowed to*** *stay up late in the week.*	*present: can, may* und *am/is/are allowed to*
Under-12s ***couldn't/weren't allowed to*** *see the film without an adult.*	*past: could* und *was/were allowed to*
*I****'ve*** *always* ***been allowed to*** *have pets.*	*present perfect: have/has been allowed to*
Will *you* ***be allowed to*** *go to the party on Friday?*	*will-future: will be allowed to*
Jeans ***must not*** *be worn at this school.* *At my school we****'re not allowed to*** *wear jeans.*	! Für **ausdrückliche Verbote** wird *must not (mustn't)* oder *be not allowed to* verwendet.

**„müssen" –
must/(to) have to**

Teacher: *You* ***must*** *work harder, Noah.* *His teacher says Noah* ***has to*** *work harder.* *I* ***needn't*** *get up at 6 tomorrow./* *I* ***don't have to*** *get up at 6 tomorrow.*	*present: must* und *have/has to* – **Verneinung:** *needn't* oder *don't/doesn't have to*
I ***had to*** *rewrite my essay.* *We* ***didn't have to*** *wait long.*	*past: had to* – **Verneinung:** *didn't have to*
Lauren ***has had to*** *go to the dentist's.*	*present perfect: have/has had to*
You ***will have to*** *go to the dentist's too if you eat so many sweets.*	*will-future: will have to*
Everyone ***needs to*** *take a break now and again.* *You* ***don't need to*** *wait for us.* *I* ***didn't need to*** *tell her. She already knew it.* ***Do*** *we* ***need*** *to book a table?*	Auch das Vollverb *(to) need to* wird verwendet, um zu sagen, dass jemand etwas tun muss oder nicht zu tun braucht.

4.3 Modal auxiliaries – what do they express?

Modale Hilfsverben können ganz unterschiedliche Dinge zum Ausdruck bringen. Mit ***can*** kannst du z. B.
- sagen, dass jemand etwas tun **kann** oder **darf**
- jemanden um etwas **bitten** oder zu etwas **auffordern**
- um **Erlaubnis bitten** oder ein **Verbot aussprechen**

usw.

Die folgenden Kästen geben dir einen Überblick.

Ability (Fähigkeit)

I ***can*** *speak French and a little German.*	Ich **kann** Französisch und ein bisschen Deutsch.
They ***could*** *hear someone in the next room.*	Sie **konnten** jemanden im Nebenzimmer hören.

Request (Bitte/Aufforderung)

Would *you help me to wash the dishes?*	**Würdest** du mir helfen abzuwaschen?
Could *you be quiet, please?*	**Kannst/Könntest** du bitte leise sein?

Permission, prohibition (Erlaubnis, Verbot)

Can/May *I use your phone, please?*	**Kann/Darf** ich mal dein Telefon benutzen, bitte?
You ***can't*** *take photos in the museum.*	Du **darfst** im Museum nicht fotografieren.
In 1968, children ***could*** *leave school at 15.*	… **konnten/durften** Kinder mit 15 die Schule verlassen.
You ***mustn't*** *tell Julie about the concert. It's a surprise.*	Du **darfst** Julie nichts von dem Konzert erzählen. …

Suggestion (Vorschlag)

Couldn't *you ask your grandma?*	**Könntest** du nicht deine Oma fragen?
You ***could*** *talk to your teacher.*	Du **könntest** (doch) mit deiner Lehrerin sprechen.
Shall *we eat first and go shopping later?*	**Sollen/Wollen** wir erst essen …?

Offer (Angebot)

Can/Could *I get you a drink?*	**Kann** ich Ihnen (vielleicht) etwas zu trinken holen?
Would *you like to stay for dinner?*	**Möchten** Sie (nicht) zum Essen bleiben?
Shall *I help you with the dishes?*	**Soll** ich dir beim Abwasch helfen?

Refusal, rejection (Weigerung, Ablehnung)

My father ***won't*** *let me stay out after ten.*	Mein Vater **will nicht**, dass ich nach zehn noch draußen bin.
I can't get in. The gate ***won't*** *open.*	… Das Tor **will nicht** aufgehen/geht nicht auf.
He knew the answer, but he ***wouldn't*** *tell me.*	…, aber er **wollte** sie mir **nicht** sagen/ …, aber er weigerte sich, sie mir zu sagen.

Necessity (Notwendigkeit)

You ***needn't*** *tell Mel about the concert. She already knows.*	Du **brauchst** Mel **nicht** von dem Konzert zu erzählen. …
I've got a temperature. I ***must*** *stay in bed.*	Ich habe Fieber. Ich **muss** im Bett bleiben.

Obligation, advice (Verpflichtung, Ratschlag)

Dogs ***should*** *be left outside.*	Hunde **sollten** draußen gelassen werden/draußen bleiben.
You ***should*** *tell him the truth./You* ***ought to*** *tell him the truth.*	Du **solltest** ihm die Wahrheit sagen.

NEW

„sollen"

*You****'re not supposed to*** *use mobiles in the theatre.*
*You****'d better*** *(= had better) turn it off.*
Man **soll** im Theater keine Handys benutzen.
Du **solltest** es (lieber) ausschalten.

*I****'d better*** *go now. It's late.*
*It's cold. You****'d better*** *not go out.*

*You****'re supposed to*** *take off your hat when you enter a church.*

The Carpenters ***are supposed to*** *be very rich.*
*They****'re said to*** *have six houses.*
Die Carpenters **sollen** sehr reich sein.
Sie **sollen** sechs Häuser haben./
Man sagt, sie hätten sechs Häuser.

Carrots ***are supposed to*** *be good for your eyes.*

Auch *had better* und *be supposed to* können für das deutsche „sollen" verwendet werden:

- *had better* ist stärker als *should* und *ought to;* es bringt zum Ausdruck, was jemand in einer bestimmten Situation am besten tun sollte.
- *be supposed to* drückt aus, dass etwas von jemandem erwartet wird bzw. wurde – z. B. weil etwas vereinbart wurde, oder weil Regeln, Traditionen oder Gesetze es verlangen.

be supposed to oder *be said to* werden auch verwendet, wenn etwas (angeblich) der Fall sein soll („die Leute sagen", „man sagt").

Possibility, probability, deduction (Möglichkeit, Wahrscheinlichkeit, Schlussfolgerung)

That ***must*** *be Luke.*	Das **muss** Luke sein.
– No, it ***can't*** *be Luke. Luke is in Spain.*	– Nein, das **kann nicht** Luke sein. Luke ist in Spanien.
Where's Dad? – He ***could*** *be at Grandma's.*	… – Er **könnte** bei Oma sein.
They ***may/might*** *still be alive.*	Sie sind **vielleicht** noch am Leben/**könnten** noch am Leben sein.
Kathy ***should*** *be/****ought to*** *be here by now.*	Kathy **sollte** jetzt (eigentlich) hier sein.
There's somebody at the door. – That ***will*** *be Sue.*	Es ist jemand an der Tür. – Das **wird** Sue sein.
That ***can't*** *have been easy.*	Das **kann nicht** einfach gewesen sein.
They ***must*** *have fallen asleep.*	Sie **müssen** eingeschlafen sein.

GF 5 The *to*-infinitive ➜ SB (pp. 162–163)

5.1 Verb + object + *to*-infinitive

*Our teacher **allows** **us** **to use** mobiles.*
… erlaubt uns, Handys zu benutzen.

*My sister **asked** **me** **not to wear** her T-shirts.*
… bat mich, nicht ihre T-Shirts zu tragen.

*Pictures can **help** **you** **to understand** new words.*
Bilder können dir helfen, neue Wörter zu verstehen.

*The police officer **told** **us** **to wait** outside.*
… sagte, dass wir draußen warten sollten./
… forderte uns auf, draußen zu warten.

*The hurricane **caused** **the house** **to collapse**.*
Der Hurrikan bewirkte, dass das Haus zusammenbrach./
… verursachte den Zusammenbruch des Hauses.

*His parents **expect/want** **him** **to be** home by ten.*
… erwarten/wollen, dass er um zehn zu Hause ist.

*I'**d like** **you** **to sit** down in a circle now.*
Ich möchte, dass ihr euch jetzt im Kreis hinsetzt.

Nach bestimmten Verben kann ein **Objekt** + ***to*-Infinitiv** stehen. Beispiele:
allow/ask/help/invite/teach sb. to do sth.

Im Deutschen steht meist ein Inifinitiv mit „zu":
jm. erlauben/jn. bitten/jm. helfen/jn. einladen/ jm. beibringen, etwas zu tun

Auch nach den Verben ***cause, expect, tell, want, would like, would love*** kann ein **Objekt + *to*-Infinitiv** stehen.

! Nach den entsprechenden deutschen Verben steht meist ein Nebensatz mit „dass", aber auf die englischen Verben darf **kein *that*-Satz** folgen:

Deutsch: *Ich **möchte/erwarte**, **dass er uns hilft**.*

Englisch: *I **want** **him**/I **expect** **him to help us**.*
Nicht: ~~*I want/expect that he*~~ …

5.2 Question word + *to*-infinitive

*Can you tell me **how to get** to the station?*
Können Sie mir sagen, wie ich zum Bahnhof komme/ kommen kann?

*I don't know **what to do**.*
Ich weiß nicht, was ich tun soll.

*I need help, but I don't know **who to ask**.*
Ich brauche Hilfe, aber ich weiß nicht, wen ich fragen kann/soll.

*We had no idea **where to go**.*
Wir hatten keine Ahnung, wohin wir gehen sollten.

Der ***to*-Infinitiv** steht oft nach einem **Fragewort** (*what, who, how, when, where* usw.). Er entspricht in der Regel einem Nebensatz mit modalem Hilfsverb (*can, could, should* usw.).

Vergleiche: *I don't know who to ask.*
I don't know who I can ask/who I should ask.

Die Kombination aus Fragewort und *to*-Infinitiv steht oft nach den Verben *ask, explain, find out, know, show, tell, wonder.*

5.3 The *to*-infinitive instead of a relative clause

***The first/last (person)** **to arrive** was Jonathan.*
(The first/last person who arrived …)

*We're **the only shop** **to offer** this service.*
(… the only shop that offers this service)

*Ava was **the only person/the only one** **to tell** the truth.*
(… the only person/the only one who told …)

*Sophie was **the youngest (girl)** **to take** part.*
(… the youngest girl who took part)

*Philip is **the person** **to ask** about computers.*
*(… the person who you **should** ask …)*

*Luigi's is **the place** **to go** for a good pizza.*
*(… the place that you **must/should** go to …)*

*I'm looking for **someone** **to share** a flat with.*
*(… someone who I **can** share a flat with)*

*Lily doesn't know **anybody** **to play** with.*
*(… anybody who she **can/could** play with)*

In den folgenden Fällen entspricht der *to*-Infinitiv einem **Relativsatz**:
- nach ***the first, the last, the next, the only***

! Nach *the only* muss ein Nomen oder *one/ones* stehen.

- nach einem **Superlativ**
- nach einen **Nomen** (besonders häufig nach ***person, place, way***) und nach **Zusammensetzungen mit *some-*, *any-*** und ***no-*** (*someone, something, anybody, nowhere, …*)

In diesen Fällen entspricht der *to*-Infinitiv einem **Relativsatz mit modalem Hilfsverb**.

GF 6 Conditional sentences ➔ SB (pp. 164–165)

Subordinate clause	Main clause
If you give me your number,	*I'll call you.*
Wenn du mir deine Nummer gibst,	rufe ich dich an.

Bedingungssätze („Wenn …, dann …"-Sätze) bestehen aus einem **Hauptsatz** *(main clause)* und einem **Nebensatz** *(subordinate clause)* mit ***if*** („wenn/falls").

if + present — *will*-future

If I ***miss*** *the bus,* — *I****'ll take*** *a taxi.*

Wenn ich den Bus **verpasse**, **nehme** ich ein Taxi.

If Dan ***misses*** *the bus, he* ***can/should/must take*** *a taxi.*

If you ***miss*** *the bus,* ***take*** *a taxi.*

Typ 1 („Was ist, wenn …"-Sätze)

Diese Bedingungssätze beziehen sich auf die **Gegenwart** oder die **Zukunft**. Sie drücken aus, was unter bestimmten Bedingungen **geschieht/geschehen wird** oder **nicht geschieht/nicht geschehen wird**.

Statt des Futurs mit ***will*** können im Hauptsatz auch die modalen Hilfsverben ***can, should, must*** usw. oder ein **Imperativ** stehen.

if + past — *would* + infinitive

If I ***missed*** *the bus,* — *I****'d*** *(= I* ***would****)* ***take*** *a taxi.*

Wenn ich den Bus **verpasste/verpassen würde**, **würde** ich ein Taxi **nehmen**.

If Dan ***missed*** *the bus, he* ***could/might take*** *a taxi.*

Typ 2 („Was wäre, wenn …"-Sätze)

Auch diese Bedingungssätze beziehen sich auf die **Gegenwart** oder die **Zukunft**. Sie drücken aus, was unter bestimmten Bedingungen **geschehen** oder **nicht geschehen würde**.

Statt ***would*** können im Hauptsatz auch ***could*** oder ***might*** + Infinitiv stehen.

NEW

if + past perfect — *would have* + past participle

If I ***had missed*** *the bus,* — *I* ***would have taken*** *a taxi.*

Wenn ich den Bus **verpasst hätte**, **hätte** ich ein Taxi **genommen**.

If Dan ***had missed*** *the bus, he* ***could have taken****/ he* ***might have taken*** *a taxi.*

Typ 3 („Was wäre gewesen, wenn …"-Sätze)

Diese Bedingungssätze beziehen sich auf die **Vergangenheit**. Sie drücken aus, was unter bestimmten Bedingungen **geschehen oder nicht geschehen wäre**.

Der *if*-Satz nennt eine Bedingung, die **nicht** eingetreten ist *(Ich habe nicht den Bus verpasst)*. Der Sprecher stellt sich nur vor, was geschehen wäre, aber in Wirklichkeit nicht geschehen ist *(Ich hätte ein Taxi genommen)*.

Statt ***would have*** können im Hauptsatz auch ***could have*** oder ***might have*** + *past participle* stehen.

If I ***knew*** *her better, I* ***would have asked*** *her.*
Wenn ich sie besser kennen würde, hätte ich sie gefragt.
*If you****'ve been*** *here before, you****'ll know*** *the rules.*
Wenn du schon mal hier warst, dann kennst du (ja) die Regeln.
If they ***left*** *at seven, they* ***won't be*** *here until twelve.*
Wenn sie um sieben losgefahren sind, werden sie nicht vor zwölf hier sein.

Ähnlich wie im Deutschen werden in englischen Bedingungssätzen – je nach Situation – auch andere Kombinationen von Zeitformen verwendet als die oben beschriebenen.

Sieh dir die Beispiele und ihre Übersetzungen an.

GF 7 Relative clauses ➔ SB (pp. 165–167)

7.1 Defining relative clauses

1 *Do you know* <u>*the girl*</u> ***who/that works at the Oxfam shop****?*
Kennst du das Mädchen, das im Oxfam-Shop arbeitet?

2 *That's* <u>*the shop*</u> ***which/that sells second-hand clothes and books and stuff****.*
Das ist der Laden, der gebrauchte Kleidung und Bücher und so etwas verkauft.

Bestimmende Relativsätze werden mit **Relativpronomen** eingeleitet:
Bei **Personen** verwendet man die Relativpronomen ***who*** oder ***that*** **(1)**.

Bei **Dingen** verwendet man die Relativpronomen ***which*** oder ***that*** **(2)**.

Ein bestimmender Relativsatz gibt Informationen, die **zum Verständnis des Satzes notwendig** sind:
Ohne die Relativsätze … <u>*who/that works at the Oxfam shop*</u> bzw. … <u>*which/that sells second-hand clothes …*</u> wüsste man gar nicht, von welchem Mädchen bzw. von welchem Geschäft die Rede ist.
Anders als im Deutschen werden solche Relativsätze nicht durch Kommas abgetrennt.

7.2 Contact clauses

1 *Mr Jones is the teacher **who I like the most**.*
***or**: Mr Jones is the teacher **I like the most**.*

2 *These are the photos **that Dad took in Wales**.*
***or**: These are the photos **Dad took in Wales**.*

3 *Who was the man **who was talking** to Jeremy at the bus stop?*

Wenn das Relativpronomen **Objekt des Relativsatzes** ist, wird es oft weggelassen **(1, 2)**.
Relativsätze ohne Relativpronomen werden ***contact clauses*** genannt.

! Wenn das **Relativpronomen direkt vor dem Verb** steht, ist es **Subjekt** und darf **nicht** weggelassen werden **(3)**.

Vergleiche:
– *… the man **who was talking to** Jeremy*
(„… der Mann, **der** mit Jeremy gesprochen hat")
– *… the man **who Jeremy was talking to*** oder
*… the man **Jeremy was talking to***
(„… der Mann, mit dem **Jeremy** gesprochen hat")

7.3 Non-defining relative clauses

*Agatha Christie**, who died in 1976,** wrote about 70 detective novels and 17 plays.*

*John Lennon, **whose mother taught him to play the banjo in the 1950s,** later became world-famous as a member of the Beatles.*

*At 11.35 we landed at Atlanta International**, which is one of the world's busiest airports**.*

Nicht bestimmende Relativsätze kommen hauptsächlich in geschriebenem Englisch vor. Sie geben **Zusatzinformationen**, die man nicht unbedingt braucht, um zu verstehen, von wem oder was die Rede ist: Man versteht den Satz *Agatha Christie wrote about 70 detective novels* auch ohne den Relativsatz *who died in 1976*.

!
- In nicht bestimmenden Relativsätzen darf man das **Relativpronomen nie weglassen**.
- Es können nur die Relativpronomen *who*, *which* und *whose* verwendet werden – nicht aber *that*.
- Nicht bestimmende Relativsätze werden durch **Kommas** abgetrennt.

7.4 Relative clauses with *which* to refer to a whole clause

*In December 1980, John Lennon was murdered**, which shocked people all over the world**.*
…, was Menschen auf der ganzen Welt schockierte.

*Our neighbours helped us to tidy up after the party**, which I think was very good of them**.*
…, was ich sehr nett von ihnen fand.

*We're moving to Leeds in the summer**, which means I'll have to change school**.*
…, was bedeutet, dass ich die Schule wechseln muss.

Relativsätze mit ***which*** können sich auch auf einen ganzen Satz beziehen. Sie kommentieren die Aussage im vorausgehenden Hauptsatz.

Im Deutschen werden solche Relativsätze mit „was" eingeleitet.

Satzbezogene Relativsätze werden durch **Kommas** abgetrennt.

GF 8 Participles ➜ *SB (pp. 167–170)*

8.1 Participle forms

Present participle: *-ing*

work	→ ***working***	*try*	→ ***trying***
dance	→ ***dancing***	*plan*	→ ***planning***

Past participle, regular verbs: *-ed*

work	→ ***worked***	*try*	→ ***tried***
dance	→ ***danced***	*plan*	→ ***planned***

Past participle, irregular verbs:

build	→ ***built***	*grow*	→ ***grown***
make	→ ***made***	*see*	→ ***seen***
teach	→ ***taught***	*write*	→ ***written***

Das **Partizip Präsens** *(present participle)* wird bei allen Verben durch Anhängen von ***-ing*** an den Infinitiv gebildet. Beachte die Besonderheiten bei der Schreibung.

Das **Partizip Perfekt** *(past participle)* von **regelmäßigen Verben** bildet man durch Anhängen von ***-ed*** an den Infinitiv.

Unregelmäßige Verben haben eigene *past participle*-Formen, die man einzeln lernen muss.

➜ *Unregelmäßige Verben: SB, S. 240–241*

8.2 Participle clauses instead of relative clauses

The city is always full of people ***who are looking for a parking space****.*
→ *… full of people* ***looking for a parking space****.*
… voller Menschen, die nach einem Parkplatz suchen.

The man ***who was driving the red car*** *waved at us.*
→ *The man* ***driving the red car*** *waved at us.*

The Eurovision Song Contest is an international competition ***which is watched by millions of people****.*
→ *… competition* ***watched by millions of people****.*
… Wettbewerb, der … angeschaut wird.

Relativsätze werden oft zu einem sogenannten **Partizipialsatz** verkürzt.

Das ***present participle*** entspricht dabei einem Relativpronomen + Verb im **Aktiv**. Vergleiche:
… people ***looking*** *for a parking space*
… people ***who are looking*** *for a parking space*

Das ***past participle*** entspricht einem Relativpronomen + Verb im **Passiv**. Vergleiche:
… competition ***watched*** *by millions of people*
… competition ***which is watched*** *by millions of people*

8.3 Verb of perception + object + present participle

	Verb of perception	Object	Present participle	
1 *We*	***heard***	***a baby***	***crying****.*	
2 *She*	***saw***	***someone***	***climbing***	*on the roof.*
3 *He*	***watched***	***the band***	***getting***	*ready for the show.*
4 *I*	***noticed***	***two women***	***arguing***	*outside the hotel.*

1 Wir hörten ein Baby weinen.
2 Sie sah jemanden auf das Dach klettern./ …, wie/dass jemand auf das Dach kletterte.
3 Er beobachtete, wie sich die Band für die Show bereitmachte.
4 Ich bemerkte zwei Frauen, die sich vorm Hotel stritten./ …, dass sich zwei Frauen … stritten.

Auf Verben der Wahrnehmung wie ***feel, hear, listen to, notice, see, smell, spot, watch*** kann ein **Objekt** + **Partizip Präsens** folgen.

Mit solchen Sätzen sagt man, dass man etwas wahrnimmt, das gerade im Gang ist (bzw. war).

Im Deutschen steht in diesen Fällen meist ein Infinitiv oder ein Nebensatz mit „wie“ oder „dass“, manchmal auch ein Relativsatz.

(Wenn man betonen will, dass man ein Geschehen **vollständig** – **von Anfang bis Ende** – wahrgenommen hat, verwendet man statt des *present participle* einen **Infinitiv**:
We ***saw him grab*** *the money and* ***run*** *away.*
Wir sahen, wie er sich das Geld schnappte und davonlief.)

8.4 Participle clauses giving additional information

NEW

It rains a lot here, ***sometimes flooding the roads****.*
Hier regnet es viel, und manchmal überschwemmt es (dabei) die Straßen.

Last Sunday morning, we stayed in bed, ***reading and listening to the radio****.*
Letzten Sonntagmorgen sind wir im Bett geblieben und haben gelesen und Radio gehört.

Charlotte ran down the stairs, ***losing a shoe****.*
…, wobei sie einen Schuh verlor.

Using a knife*, she was able to open the door.*
Indem sie ein Messer benutzte, …

Partizipialsätze mit *present participle* werden oft verwendet, um **Zusatzinformationen** zu geben oder **Begleitumstände** einer Handlung zu beschreiben.
(Meist handelt es sich um zeitgleich oder fast zeitgleich stattfindende Handlungen oder Vorgänge.)

Im Deutschen steht meist ein Hauptsatz mit „und“, machmal auch ein Nebensatz mit „wobei“ oder „indem“.

He stood in front of the audience, wishing he was somewhere else.
Er stand vor dem Publikum und wünschte sich, woanders zu sein.

8.5 Participle clauses instead of adverbial clauses of time

NEW

***When planning* a trip to a foreign country,** *start early and ask people who have been there.*
Wenn du eine Reise in ein fremdes Land planst, …

***While walking* down the street,** *I saw a huge black dog.*
Als/Während ich die Straße hinunterging, …

***When asked* why he left school so early,** *he answered that he wanted to earn his own money.*
Als er gefragt wurde, …

Always be polite ***when asking* for information.**
…, wenn du um Informationen bittest.

Partizipialsätze, die mit *when* oder *while* eingeleitet sind, entsprechen **Nebensätzen der Zeit**.

Das ***present participle*** entspricht dabei wieder einem Verb im **Aktiv** *(while walking = while I was walking)*.
Das ***past participle*** entspricht einem Verb im **Passiv** *(when asked = when he was asked)*.

Oft gehen solche Partizipialsätze dem Hauptsatz voran. Sie sind typisch für das geschriebene Englisch.

***Walking* down the street,** *I saw a huge black dog.*
Als/Während ich die Straße hinunterging, …

***Asked* why he left school so early,** *he answered that he wanted to earn his own money.*
Als er gefragt wurde, …

Manchmal wird bei Partizipialsätzen anstelle von Nebensätzen der Zeit die Konjunktion weggelassen.

1a *Joe met an old friend* ***while* looking for a job.**
(= Joe met an old friend while he – Joe – was looking for a job)
…, während er auf der Suche nach einer Stelle war.

1b *Joe met an old friend* **looking for a job.**
(= Joe met an old friend who was looking for a job)
…, der auf der Suche nach einer Stelle war.

! Vorsicht! Wenn der Partizipialsatz auf den Hauptsatz folgt, musst du aufpassen.
Vergleiche die Sätze **1a** und **1b**:
- In **1a** ist es Joe, der eine Stelle suchte.
- In **1b** ist es der Freund, der eine Stelle suchte.

We saw three seals ***while walking*** *along the beach.*

We saw three seals ***walking*** *along the beach.*

8.6 Participle clauses instead of adverbial clauses of reason

NEW

***Feeling* very tired,** *I decided to go to bed early.*
Weil/Da ich sehr müde war, …

***Being* a doctor,** *she knew exactly what to do.*
Weil/Da sie Ärztin ist, …

***Warned* by his wife,** *the man was able to escape.*
Weil er von seiner Frau gewarnt wurde, …/
Von seiner Frau gewarnt, …

Partizipialsätze können auch **Nebensätzen des Grundes** entsprechen.

! Beachte, dass die Konjunktion *because* nicht in Partizipialsätzen verwendet werden kann. Also nicht:

~~*Because feeling very tired*~~, …
~~*Because being a doctor*~~, …

8.7 Other participle clauses

***Although asked* to stop by the police,** *he drove on.*
Obwohl er von der Polizei aufgefordert wurde, …

You will have to wait outside ***until asked* to enter.**
…, bis Sie gebeten werden einzutreten.

***If posted* before 12 o'clock,** *the letter should arrive tomorrow.*
Wenn der Brief vor 12 Uhr eingeworfen wird, …

***After winning* gold,** *she decided to resign.*
Nachdem sie die Goldmedaille gewonnen hatte, …

Partizipialsätze können auch durch andere Konjunktionen eingeleitet werden, z. B. durch ***although, until, if, after, before***.

Checkpoint 1

1 WORDS Australia and the UK

though, vast, mainly rural, overcrowded, share, settled, convicts, Back then, Aboriginal, exchanges, Aussies, abroad, flight, easy-going, scenic, exotic, historical, mild, landmarks

2 AusE pronunciation

1 What time did your flight get in last night?
2 I bought a better pair of boots for when it gets wetter.
3 We can't see the trees very easily from here.
4 I must write a birthday card to my father this afternoon.

3 An Aussie in London

Being, visited, taking, forgetting, walking, filming, coming, believing, pulling, helping, cheering, clapping, turning, asked

4 What are they doing?

1 A 2 C

5 A conversation at the beach

a) B

b) 1 Singapore, London, Edinburgh 2 26 and a half 3 it will be colder there 4 can chat online, brother will visit 5 his dog (Rex) 6 1892 7 their accent is difficult 8 they are/were police officers 9 go to school, do homework, help at home, be polite 10 16,950

Checkpoint 2

1 WORDS Refugee Action NZ

(1) organization, (2) adapt to, (3) confused, (4) frightened, (5) familiar, (6) communication, (7) face, (8) because of, (9) cultural, (10) advisors, (11) get used to, (12) useful, (13) hopeful

2 Auckland is supposed to be worth a visit

1 (1) ought to/should, (2) are supposed to
2 (3) should/ought to/had better
3 (4) aren't supposed to, (5) had better
4 (6) should/ought to/had better
5 (7) should/ought to/had better, (8) is supposed to
6 (9) should/ought to, (10) should/ought to

3 NZ tourist places

b) 1 the gold rush
2 in sub-tropical forests/in the Bay of Islands

4 A New Zealand tradition that's all about …

a) 1 what: haka = dance by Maori people, why: to intimidate enemies 2 perform haka before international matches and competitions (since 1905) 3 feel scared 4 more than 20 million views 5 remember soldiers killed in Afghanistan, funeral of a school teacher, remember firefighters killed on 9/11 6 American football

b) frightening – angsteinjagend, warriors – Kämpfer, intimidate – einschüchtern, joy – Freude, more widely known – bekannter, challenge their opponents – ihre Gegner herausfordern, honour their comrades – ihre Kameraden ehren, around the globe – rund um den Globus

Checkpoint 3

1 WORDS Describing character

a) 1 honest 2 competitive 3 hard-working 4 tough 5 self-confident

b) 1 irresponsible 2 dishonest 3 intolerant 4 impolite 5 impatient 6 unemotional 7 unkind 8 irregular 9 disrespectful

2 What's going to happen?

1 The plane is going to land. 2 They are going to cross the street. 3 He/She is going to jump into the swimming pool.

3 What are you going to do in the holidays?

1 'm going to …, 'm not going to … 2 'll …, won't … 3 'll/won't …

4 How to write a formal letter

address, on the right, Dear Sir or Madam, Dear Mr/Mrs/Ms, short, conclusion, Yours sincerely

5 Applying for a UK job

a) youth development, competent, responsible assistants for summer camp for 4–6 weeks, work with children (8–12), creative, reliable, able to keep discipline within the groups, outdoors: physically fit, water sports, climbing and team sports, fluent in English, work experience if possible, accommodation in host families

b) siehe Aufgabe 4: How to write a formal letter

Checkpoint 4

1 WORDS Chat at the airport

native language, gap, scholarship, myself understood, slow down, backpackers, overhead lockers, space, flight attendant, itinerary, accommodation

2 Travel talk

left for/went to, left from, get on, went on, Going by, get off

3 Cycling in Vancouver

1 12, yes 2 400 hectares of green space, a mix of gardens and rain forest, aquarium, on the sea/beach, decorations made by the native people 3 oldest part of the city, small streets with shops/restaurants/trees/flowers, was founded by a British immigrant 4 Granville Island/market, Lions Gate Bridge, Coal Harbour/whale watching tours 5 70 dollars, guide/ferry/helmet, but no lunch

4 German youth hostels

1 You have to become a member of *Deutsches Jugendherbergswerk* or get an international guest ticket.
2 You have to keep your rooms tidy, help with the dishes, recycle your waste, save energy and water, you are not allowed to eat in your room, smoking and drinking are not allowed, you are not allowed to bring animals, you have to be quiet between 10 pm and 7 am.
3 You have to leave before 10 am if you haven't spoken to the manager before.